Calling
Out
the
Called

Calling Out the Called

Discipling Those Called to Ministry Leadership

SCOTT PACE
SHANE PRUITT

B&H
PUBLISHING
NASHVILLE, TENNESSEE

Copyright © 2022 by R. Scott Pace and Shane Pruitt
All rights reserved.
Printed in the United States of America

978-1-0877-6982-0

Published by B&H Publishing Group
Nashville, Tennessee

Dewey Decimal Classification: 254
Subject Heading: LEADERSHIP / MINISTRY /
MINISTERS—CALLING AND TRAINING

Cover design by Darren Welch.

2 3 4 5 6 7 • 26 25 24 23 22

To all the faithful servants who are calling out and discipling
those called to ministry leadership.

Acknowledgments

In challenging others to consider their calling, it's impossible to not reflect on my experience as family, friends, and leaders challenged me to explore and discern my own calling. I'm thankful for the heart for Christ that my parents cultivated within me that ultimately prepared me to answer God's call to vocational ministry. I'm deeply grateful for the spiritual and ministry influence of men like Bill Bennett, Danny Akin, Stephen Rummage, and Jim Shaddix who have helped equip me to fulfill my calling. Ministry isn't possible without God's people and the Lord has encouraged, affirmed, and refined my calling through so many saints in the churches I've been privileged to serve. Thank you!

I have the joy of working each day alongside the faculty and family of Southeastern Baptist Theological Seminary who are dedicated to equipping students to serve the church and fulfill the Great Commission. Their dedication to develop and deploy leaders helped inspire my contribution to this project and I thank the Lord daily for their formative role in my life.

I'm thankful for the team at Lifeway and B&H who have been instrumental in supporting the vision for this project from its inception. Thank you to the publishing staff who have worked so diligently to help it come to fruition. Your commitment to excellence and your gracious spirit have made the process a joy!

Most of all, I'm grateful for my wife, Dana, for her strength and support that enables me to fulfill my ministry calling. The joy of partnering in marriage and ministry with you as we serve the Lord together is the greatest privilege of my life. I'm certain God's calling for our four beautiful children will be largely discerned through your faithful love and tireless service to our family!

To my beloved Savior and exalted King, Jesus Christ: may you receive the honor and glory for any fruit born by this labor of love given as an offering to you!

Scott Pace

Wake Forest, North Carolina

My wife Kasi and our six children—Raygen, Harper, Titus, Morris, Elliot, and Glory: I pray you always feel valued, loved, and ministered to by me. You are my primary ministry.

Mom and Dad: You have been a constant source of inspiration and encouragement for me.

My wife's family—Tommy and Kelly, Poppy (who is now with Jesus) and Meemaw, and Rex: Thank you for making me part of the family from day one.

Kevin Ezell: I am also so thankful for your leadership and friendship in my life. It's an honor and privilege to serve under your leadership. Thank you for your sacred trust in me to serve our churches in North America.

Our friends who have become like family to us: You know who you are. Kasi and I constantly thank our great God for surrounding us with such an awesome community of people.

Taylor Combs, Logan Pyron, and Scott Pace: I am forever indebted to you because this book would not be possible without you.

Shane Pruitt
Rockwall, Texas

Contents

Calling Out the Callers

Hard Questions and Honest Answers

Have you ever had a sinking feeling that a big problem is lurking around the corner? Maybe you've noticed drops of oil on your garage floor or a growing water stain on your ceiling. These scenarios are examples of small symptoms behind much larger problems. Whether they are the result of unintentional oversights or reveal negligence on our part, you can be certain that the cost and collateral damage will be far greater if you don't confront the issue head-on.

In many ways, we face a similar situation related to ministry leadership. Concerning indicators demand our attention. In 1992, Barna reported that the median age for Protestant pastors was forty-four. Approximately one-third of pastors were under the age of forty, and more than 75 percent of pastors were under the age of fifty-five. Twenty-five years later, in 2017, Barna revealed that the median age had increased to fifty-four with only 50 percent of pastors being younger than fifty-five. Perhaps the most staggering number was the steep decline of pastors under the age of forty that plummeted to less than 15 percent! As David Kinnaman, president of Barna Research, observed, these numbers represent a "substantial crisis" since "there are now more full-time senior pastors over the age of sixty-five than under the age of forty."[1]

Although a variety of dynamics contribute to these concerning trends, the combination of a reduced emphasis on ministerial calling and a corresponding lack of interest among younger believers are two of the primary factors. Supporting Barna's results, Lifeway Research reported that 70 percent of pastors believe young leaders view "other kinds of work" as more important than vocational ministry, and 69 percent of pastors indicated that it is becoming increasingly difficult to find mature young Christians who aspire to be in vocational ministry.[2]

These statistics go well beyond the caution level of oil drops and water stains. They are blaring alarms of the catastrophic consequences if we fail to address them with anything less than a zealous and concerted effort. In response to these alarming trends, Kinnaman concludes, "It is urgent that denominations, networks and independent churches determine how to best motivate, mobilize, resource and deploy more younger pastors."[3] In other words, we must renew our commitment to passionately and persistently "calling out the called"!

But before we do, we must consider three foundational aspects of the conversation: (1) the concept of "calling" and what we believe about its nature; (2) the current state of the ministry landscape, including obstacles and objections to promoting a ministerial calling; and (3) practical ways we can cultivate a ministry climate that helps people discern a call to ministry. Three questions will help us address each of these foundational issues.

How Should We Think about Calling?

To answer this question, we must begin by asking and answering the question of whether a "call to ministry" even exists. As you reflect on your own personal testimony (or current ministry position!), that probing thought may create some angst. But we cannot afford to build a conversation on a presumed premise that is largely based on conventional thought or subjective experience. Therefore, we must look to the Scriptures to determine if God calls some people to vocational ministry.

Throughout the Bible, God has identified and set apart certain individuals for specific purposes. Old Testament examples abound, including Noah (Gen. 6), Abram (Gen. 12), Moses (Exod. 3), Deborah (Judges 4), Samuel (1 Sam. 3), David (1 Sam. 16), Nehemiah (Neh. 1), Esther (Esther 4), Isaiah (Isa. 6), Jeremiah (Jer. 1), and countless other prophets, priests, and kings. Hebrews 11 recounts even more testimonies of those who played a particular role within God's redemptive plan, including those who lack substantial notoriety. Likewise, the New Testament includes strategically appointed individuals, such as the twelve apostles (Matt. 10), Steven (Acts 7), Philip (Acts 8), Saul (Acts 9), Barnabas (Acts 11), Silas (Acts 15), Lydia (Acts 16), Phoebe (Rom. 16), Epaphroditus

(Phil. 3), and a variety of other faithful servants of varying levels of recognition mentioned throughout the epistles.

While this assures us that God uses everyday individuals to accomplish his extraordinary plans, these biblical examples by themselves do not definitively validate the notion of a ministerial calling. However, the personal nature of God's will that these testimonies demonstrate is a crucial part of the concept.

In additional to the individual purpose God has for each of his people, there is also biblical precedent for those who are set apart specifically for the purpose of spiritual service and leadership. In the Old Testament, prophets were designated to declare the word of the Lord to God's people and were also set apart for God's spiritual purposes. For example, Jeremiah's testimony affirms that he was chosen, "set apart," and "appointed" as a "prophet to the nations" (Jer. 1:5). Likewise, Aaron and his sons (the Levites) were chosen to serve the Lord as priests in the tabernacle and temple (Exod. 28–29; Num. 18:2–6).

Another appointed office of spiritual leadership in the Old Testament was the king. Although his role could not supersede the work of priests (1 Sam. 13), kings were responsible for the spiritual health of God's people and were intended to lead them according to God's law. King Josiah exhibited this godly leadership in implementing his spiritual reforms that renewed God's covenant with his people (2 Kings 23). These offices were God's representatives who ultimately foreshadowed Jesus as the true Prophet, Priest, and King.

Similarly, in the New Testament, the Lord designated spiritual leaders for his covenant people. God provided personified gifts (i.e., pastors, evangelists, teachers) to the church "to equip the saints for the work of ministry" and "to build up the body of Christ" (Eph. 4:11–12). It is also noteworthy that the offices of church leadership, pastors and deacons, have prescribed standards that reserve them for appointed individuals (1 Tim. 3:8–13; 1 Tim. 1:5–9). And Peter provided specific instruction to church elders regarding their designated responsibility to "shepherd God's flock" (1 Pet. 5:1–4). In doing so, these spiritual leaders ultimately represent Jesus, the chief Shepherd and Overseer (1 Pet. 2:25; 5:4), as they serve and minister to God's people.

While these passages do not limit spiritual leadership to a particular office or role, they effectively demonstrate the reality of qualified individuals set apart to serve in specific ministerial capacities. In addition, Scripture affirms the vocational nature of such roles by compensating those who dedicate their lives to spiritual service and leadership. In the Old Testament, the Levites were supported through designated provisions (Num. 18:21) while the New Testament advocates for spiritual leaders to receive financial support from the church (1 Cor. 9:6–12; 1 Tim. 5:17–18).

The combination of God's individual purpose for believers, designated spiritual leadership among his people, and affirmation of vocational service capacities collectively support the concept of ministerial calling. But the "call" must also be affirmed as that which can be personally discerned as God's purpose for certain individuals to surrender their lives to vocational ministry.

While those who are "called" typically refers to all believers (Jude 1:1; 1 Cor. 1:2), the gracious salvation we all share (1 Cor. 1:9), and God's sanctifying purpose for all of his people (1 Thess. 4:3, 7), other scriptural references affirm the ministerial aspect of "calling" as well. For instance, the author of Hebrews references Aaron's role as a priest not as one that he assumed but one he was assigned and *"called* by God" to perform (Heb. 5:4, emphasis added). Likewise, he refers to Abraham's faith and obedience to follow God's plan "when he was *called"* (Heb. 11:8, emphasis added).

Paul speaks of his own experience as a calling that echoes the prophet Jeremiah's testimony, that he was "set apart" from his "mother's womb" and *"called"* by God's grace for the purpose of preaching Christ among the Gentiles (Gal. 1:15–16, emphasis added; cf. Jer. 1:5). The term Paul uses, *called,* clearly includes God's call to salvation (cf. Gal. 1:6), but it also involves a designated ministry role for which he was "set apart" within God's plan. In other letters he references his calling according to his ministerial role, identifying himself as "Paul, *called* as an apostle of Christ Jesus by God's will" (1 Cor. 1:1, emphasis added).

In his final epistle, he encourages Timothy as the young pastor of the church of Ephesus: "[God] has saved us and *called* us with a holy calling" (2 Tim. 1:9, emphasis added). And as he prepares for his impending execution, Paul clings to God's specific purpose for his life in dedication to the gospel as one who was *"appointed* a herald, apostle, and teacher" (2 Tim. 1:11, emphasis added). Correspondingly, throughout the letter Paul offers personal instruction to Timothy in his leadership role as "the Lord's servant" (2 Tim. 2:24) and exhorts him to perform his ministerial responsibilities in order to "fulfill *your* ministry" (2 Tim. 4:5, emphasis added).

While subsequent chapters will further clarify the nature of God's call to ministry, how it differs from other vocational callings, and how it can be discerned, this brief overview of biblical evidence at least provides the necessary support to validate the concept of a "call to ministry" as typically understood. It also raises some other important questions we must consider regarding the responsibility of ministry leaders in "calling out the called."

Why Don't We Teach about Calling?

In recent decades, the focus has shifted away from intentionally inviting believers to consider vocational ministry as a calling. There are a variety of reasons for this trend, and in identifying some of them, we can navigate the hurdles that have kept us from "calling out the called."

One of the primary obstacles in this endeavor has been the drift from public invitations in general. Understandably, ministry leaders want to avoid manipulation and any practice that may mislead or confuse those who sit under their teaching. But the possibility of this and even patterns of exploiting the invitation do not justify its elimination. We must be careful to trust the Spirit to work through the power of the gospel and truth of God's Word in leading hearers to respond. We should be clear instead of being clever. We should invite rather than intimidate. As we strive for balance, we must also affirm that an urgent and passionate appeal corresponds with the gravity of the gospel and does not automatically equate with spiritual coercion. Therefore, we must regularly provide opportunities for listeners to respond to the life-changing power of the gospel. And these invitations should span the full spectrum of gospel implications, from initial conversion to ministerial calling and everything in between.

Another challenge we face in "calling out the called" is the unfortunate mischaracterization of what it means to be in vocational ministry. This multifaceted obstacle includes several sources of skewed perspective. For instance, the role of ministry leaders within our communities has gone from a traditional position of respect and esteem to one of scrutiny and maligning. This results from faithful leaders who have refused to compromise the truth of God's Word by bowing to the hostility of the world and the pressure to conform. It has also resulted from the failures of prominent ministry leaders who have seemingly validated the world's persistent accusations of hypocrisy. Along with the culture celebrating these moral collapses, these instances have also disenchanted a generation of young believers within the church who now question ministry leaders, their authenticity and integrity, and wonder what it even means to be "in ministry."

In addition to the unfortunate and the unfounded obstacles, perhaps the greatest obstacle we face is an unintended one. In recent decades the desire to mobilize the church, emphasize spiritual community, and authorize every member to live on mission has essentially neutralized a call to vocational ministry. It is important for us to affirm that, indeed, in the church there is no spiritual "varsity" team of leaders and "junior varsity" team of laity. God calls all believers to serve the local church and fulfill the Great Commission. All Christians have

> It is important for us to affirm that, indeed, in the church there is no spiritual "varsity" team of leaders and "junior varsity" team of laity.

the responsibility and privilege of sharing the gospel and standing on the truth of God's Word. In this sense, there is a "universal calling" for *all* believers to serve the Lord and actively participate in his mission. So-called "secular" vocations are intended by God to be missional platforms in our culture and communities. These vocational callings are essential to the gospel mission's being accomplished!

These realities must not only be acknowledged but also asserted within the church. At the same time, we must be careful that we do not undermine the ministerial calling of some in a well-intended (and biblically accurate!) effort to affirm the value of every believer in God's kingdom. While there is a universal calling for all believers, there is also a unique calling for each individual disciple. When we consider the missional heart of our heavenly Father and the size of the task at hand, we can recognize the need for all believers, regardless of their vocational capacity, to leverage their unique calling for the cause of Christ.

> While there is a universal calling for all believers, there is also a unique calling for each individual disciple.

Jesus modeled this balanced approach. As he traveled, teaching and preaching the gospel, he was moved with compassion when he considered the lostness of the world around him. As a result, he instructed his disciples, "The harvest is abundant, but the workers are few. Therefore, pray to the Lord of the harvest to send out workers into his harvest" (Matt. 9:37–38). In the following chapter, Jesus anointed the twelve apostles and sent them out for this purpose. In the same way, we must pray for God to send out workers in all capacities to participate in the harvest while we simultaneously train and mobilize those who are called to serve in vocational roles of ministry leadership.

How Can We Talk about Calling?

If we are going to commit to calling out the called, we must also consider the practical ways we can do this in our ministries that are both biblically sound and personally responsible. While not every ministry context looks the same, some applicable principles and ongoing action points can help facilitate this work and fertilize the soil of any ministry. But it starts with a patient mindset and a humble faith that pursue more of a climate change in our ministries rather than creating lightning-strike moments. Calling should become a concept that is regularly talked about in our ministry in a variety of ways. By integrating some of these principles and practices, we can help facilitate healthy conversations with our people that can lead to prayerful consideration about their potential ministerial calling.

- ***Extend invitations.*** Perhaps the most obvious way we can cultivate this type of calling culture is to regularly include a ministerial calling and its possibility as part of our invitations for response. If our listeners are not aware or do not know that it is an option to prayerfully consider, it is difficult for them to discern this type of calling as part of God's will for their lives. Our appeals for response, in whatever form is appropriate for your context, should not only provide opportunities for people to trust Christ for salvation, but they should also invite believers to consider vocational ministry and career missions as a possibility.

- **Share testimonies.** In any situation, some of the most difficult hurdles to overcome are the fear of the unknown and the misconception of the familiar. Personal testimonies of those who have been called into vocational ministry can help our people disarm their fears and clarify their understanding to consider what full-time ministry service really involves. We should regularly refer to our calling in order to exhort all believers toward obedience and surrender, regardless of their unique calling, and to help those who may be considering a ministerial calling.

- **Celebrate the church.** Many people are conditioned to have a negative view of the church. Whether through cultural influence or personal experiences, many believers have been disappointed and have become disenchanted with the church. Beyond the church itself, sometimes we can also be guilty of bemoaning our ministry responsibilities or complaining about relational dynamics to garner sympathy and appreciation. But this cynical disposition can sour our people toward vocational ministry. While our goal should not be to shield people from the truth or promote a ministry façade, we should model a love for the church as the body and bride of Christ that is positive, affirming, and exhibits gratitude for the privilege of serving the Lord in a ministry capacity.

- *Provide opportunities.* A primary element of discerning a call to ministry involves discovering spiritual passions and gifts through service opportunities. We may be guilty, at times, of holding ministry responsibilities with a closed fist instead of an open hand. Whether the result of personal insecurity, a desire for control, a lack of trust in others, or an ego that craves credit, we must relinquish our selfish desires to encourage, enable, and empower others to do the work of the ministry. As people explore, exercise, and employ their spiritual gifts, they may also discern God's calling on their lives to serve in a similar vocational capacity.
- *Train leaders.* As we cultivate a ministry environment that cooperates with the Spirit

in calling out the called, we must be prepared to mentor those who discern a call to vocational ministry. There is no substitute for your personal involvement in their lives. In many ways the discipleship process is identical to what we would do for every follower of Christ. And yet, like any other vocational apprenticeship, particular skills, competencies, values, and character attributes are necessary for their success and are learned through experience. Whether we provide this training through a formal internship position or through an intentional mentoring relationship, we must be available to invest in these future leaders. As ministers, this is a weighty matter of personal stewardship because God entrusts us with their development as they discern, clarify, and pursue their calling.

What's Ahead?

In answering these three foundational questions, we prayerfully desire to see God burden the hearts of ministry leaders to join together in an effort to see him raise up a new generation of pastors, missionaries, and ministry leaders as workers in the harvest.

In looking ahead, it is important to recognize what this book is not intended to be. It is not meant to serve as a discipleship manual that develops the spiritual disciplines vital for every believer. Many resources can provide far greater assistance in developing holy habits and deepening a Christian walk.

Our hope is to provide you with a resource designed with future vocational ministry leaders in mind that can help equip them to be faithful to their calling. If you're currently serving in ministry, how you use this book is completely based on your own gifts and experience, those entrusted to your care, and the calling they are pursuing. If you are one who is discerning your call to ministry, we hope this book will be an encouragement to you and a toolbox that provides you with the basic knowledge and skills essential for ministry success.

CHAPTER 1

Wrestling with the Call

Despite what many people from our generation want to believe, professional wrestling has always been a form of entertainment (to put it kindly!). To my dismay and disappointment, eventually I (Scott) learned that while the action was real, everything else was fake. The story lines, the feuds, and the outlandish interviews were all staged. The outcomes for the matches were predetermined, and there was no genuine struggle for the belt. "Wrasslin'" wasn't real "wrestling" at all!

Unlike the cable TV and pay-per-view version, the struggle of wrestling with the call to ministry is real! In the process of discerning God's will for our lives, we are often thrown into an internal battle between our emotions and desires. Sometimes we'll feel the tension with friends and family. Typically we will face odds and circumstances that convince us that it's impossible. While we may wish to avoid it, wrestling with the call is essential to the discernment process. So, how should we wrestle with the call? Strangely enough, the Bible provides a great example.

In Genesis 32, Jacob was grappling with the circumstances in his life and ultimately wrestled with God. For a little background, Jacob stole his brother's birthright, fled from his father's house, and was overcome with guilt, anxiety, and shame. After being exploited by his uncle for twenty years, God called Jacob to return home. Jacob was faced with the fear of seeing his brother, Esau, who had previously sought to kill him. When Jacob appealed to God, he was confronted with God's presence in an all-night wrestling match that would define his life. Jacob's physical encounter with the Lord forced him to wrestle with the spiritual reality of his own insufficiency and his need for complete surrender. Jacob didn't fully realize it, but God was calling him to fulfill the covenant promise God made with his grandfather, Abraham. Through Jacob, whom God renamed Israel (lit. "God wrestles"), the Lord would establish his covenant people, and through Jacob's family lineage, he would one day send Jesus to be the Savior of the world.

Until that point, Jacob's life was full of deception and resistance, but God brought Jacob to a point of spiritual brokenness and submission. With one touch, God crippled Jacob, and he limped the rest of his life as an enduring reminder of his spiritual transformation. The physical defeat was never God's goal. He allowed Jacob to wrestle through the night. He didn't overwhelm or overpower Jacob by force. Instead, God brought Jacob to a point of willing surrender to him. This is the same way he wrestles with us, leading us to humbly submit, give him control, and embrace his call. But in order to get to that point, there are several important steps along the way for us to take.

Confirm Your Calling

The initial step in wrestling with the call is to confirm your calling. The confirmation process involves prayerful discernment through a variety of spiritual and practical indicators we must consider. Charles Spurgeon, a well-known pastor and preacher in the nineteenth century, identified four helpful ways to recognize a call to ministry.[1]

- ***Overwhelming desire.*** Your calling will include what Spurgeon describes as "an intense, all-absorbing desire for the work."[2] This internal passion to pursue ministry is a Spirit-led aspiration for God's work that eliminates every other vocational option as a possibility and compels us to surrender our lives to the Lord's service. *Do you have an overwhelming desire for the work of ministry?*

- ***Ministry gifts.*** Spiritual giftedness and proficiency cannot be manufactured. Natural talent and a willingness to serve are no substitute. To those God calls to the specific task of vocational service, he will grant divine gifts that include particular skills required for their role, a ministry aptitude for spiritual leadership, and a special capacity for a lifetime of service. *Do you recognize God's gifts in your life that he wants to use for his glory?*

- **God's blessing.** God's call can also be recognized through the spiritual fruit he produces through our faithful service. Spurgeon acknowledges that there may be seasons of drought, but our usefulness to the Lord will ultimately be affirmed by the spiritual harvest that comes from our labor. Spiritual birth and spiritual growth should be evident in the lives of the people we serve, providing affirmation of God's blessing and our calling. *Do you see God using you to make a spiritual difference in the lives of others?*

- **Affirmation of others.** While our goal should never be to seek the approval or applause of others, God does use the affirmation of others to confirm our calling. As we faithfully serve in the ministry opportunities God provides, his people will recognize our calling by the character they observe, the gifts that are evident, and the ways he uses us to impact the lives of others. *Do other people observe and confirm your ministry potential?*

Spurgeon's list and these reflective questions provide some helpful guidelines for us to confirm our calling. These principles are also reflected in Scripture as Paul recounted his calling to the Galatians (Gal. 1:11–24). His encounter with Jesus changed the trajectory of his life (vv. 11–14). Following his conversion (vv. 15–16), Paul confirmed his calling as an apostle through *personal affirmation* as he was compelled to preach, seek the Lord, and exercise his gifts (vv. 16–17). He also confirmed it through *private affirmation* as he consulted with Peter as one who shared his calling as an apostle (vv. 18–20). Finally, he confirmed it through *public affirmation* as the church celebrated his testimony, his preaching, and his usefulness to the Lord (vv. 21–24).[3]

Paul's example is helpful as we seek to confirm our calling, but we must also be careful to recognize that our experience may not look exactly the same. For instance, Paul's conversion and calling occurred simultaneously, but most often our calling is discerned over time through our spiritual growth and progress. It's also important to note that the specific sequence of these affirmations can vary, even though all three should be a part of our confirmation process.

Confirming your call is not easy, but it is essential. It involves wrestling with your emotions, circumstances, gifts, and desires. But without working through these things now, doubt and uncertainty will always creep in and attempt to undermine your ministry. The process of wrestling through the call is crucial because either it will release you to pursue a different vocation or it will cement your calling for seasons in ministry when you need the firm foundation of certainty and confirmation to help you persevere.

Count the Cost

Wrestling with the call also requires us to count the cost. In Luke 14:25–33, Jesus explains the level of sacrifice required to be his disciple. Because of the "great crowds" (v. 25) traveling with him, Jesus wanted to be clear that following him would require their willingness to give up everything. He elevates the supreme love for him, even beyond their own family (v. 26), and describes the crucified life involved with being his disciple (v. 27). He then illustrates his point by describing a builder who must calculate the expense of constructing a tower before starting the project (vv. 28–30) and a king who must do the same before going to war (vv. 31–32). While believers must be willing to "renounce" everything to follow Christ (v. 33), the "count the cost" principle also applies to the sacrifices that come with answering the call to ministry.

Anyone who has served in vocational ministry recognizes these realities. But sadly, many young leaders are unaware of the burdens and sacrifices that will be required. As a result, they are often disillusioned and unprepared to handle them when they come. In answering God's call, we must always count the cost.

> God's writing is an unbelievable story. Which is exactly what God loves to do.

Perhaps the most obvious cost in vocational ministry is *the heat of personal scrutiny*. The public nature of ministry requires leaders to maintain a blameless (not perfect!) lifestyle for a watching and critical world (1 Tim. 3:7). But the greatest heat ministry leaders feel most often

The first misguided motive that can be mistaken as a call to ministry is *appreciation*. When people are initially saved or when they experience a fresh work of God in their lives, naturally, gratitude flows from their hearts. It seems logical that the greatest possible way to express their appreciation is to surrender to a deeper level of service and obedience and associate this with vocational ministry. But this fails to consider how God may use them in a greater capacity from a career platform. In wrestling with the call to ministry, we must avoid the idea that vocational service is somehow more valuable to God. This mindset undermines the concept of grace by attempting to "pay him back" for all he's done in our lives. Certainly, we should be filled with thanksgiving, but appreciation for God's kindness does not equate to a call to ministry.

Another misguided motive that leads to a false sense of calling is *admiration*. When the Lord uses ministerial leaders to impact us, we can become enamored with their leadership and role. Understandably, our respect and gratitude for their personal involvement in our lives can produce a sense of obligation to "pay it forward." While passing their spiritual investment on to others is biblical (2 Tim. 2:2), it does not have to come from a position of ministry leadership. Most importantly, we must be careful that admiring our leaders does not become an unintended desire to be admired by others. In other words, sometimes it is not just the role they played but the position they occupy that becomes a dangerous motivation for pursuing a call to ministry.

One final misguided motive that must be identified and avoided is ungodly *ambition*. While we all know that we should not pursue ministry for the wrong reasons, Scripture repeatedly cautions against this reality. The apostle Peter warned leaders to guard themselves against the dangerous motives of money and power (1 Pet. 5:2–3). In the qualifications for church leaders, Scripture forbids them from being "greedy for money" (Titus 1:7; 1 Tim. 3:3). Paul repeatedly identified the gospel as the primary impetus for his service in contrast with the selfish greed and personal glory that motivated many of his ministry opponents (1 Thess. 2:3–6). Although friends or family members may discourage us from pursuing ministry because they perceive it to be a vow of poverty, some become leaders believing that "godliness is a way to material gain" (1 Tim. 6:5). In essence, these people cheapen the gospel by preaching and teaching for financial prosperity.

Like Paul, we should not focus on other people's "selfish ambition" in ministry; our chief concern should be that "Christ is proclaimed" (Phil. 1:17–18). We must, however, be careful to honestly evaluate our own motives and not pursue ministry from anything other than humble obedience to his call on our lives. If we say yes to a perceived call based on misguided motives, it only sets us up for personal disappointment that frequently includes irreparable harm to our family or the family of faith. Sadly, and even more tragically, it can also result in a leadership failure or moral collapse that brings shame to the name of Christ. So before we say yes to a call to ministry, we must check our motives and discern wisely.

Clarify Your Understanding

As we begin to sense God leading us into ministry, wrestling with our calling often raises some questions related to our future that cannot be fully or immediately answered. As a result, we can become impatient or frustrated and allow these perceived unknowns to keep us from following God's will. But instead of delaying our surrender due to an apparent lack of clarity, we should refine our expectations and clarify our understanding. Two aspects of our calling can help us address some of the common questions and the resulting confusion.

The first aspect of calling we should clarify is *direction*. When God calls us to ministry, enthusiasm and excitement breed curiosity. We want to know what the future holds, including where we will serve, what our specific ministry responsibilities will include, and how the Lord will use us. While we should be hopeful, these unknown details are not necessary to determine our next steps. When we envision these aspirational aspects of future ministry, we often create a mental image that can begin to dictate our decisions and can result in disappointment when things don't go according to our plan. Instead, we must operate more along the direction or trajectory of our calling and trust God to disclose the details along the way.

A more directional rather than detailed approach is also important to remember when we attempt to define our calling too narrowly. Many limit their calling by associating it with a specific task, being "called to preach," or a specific context, being "called to student ministry." These may, in fact, be aspects of your ministry gifts and focused efforts, but they are not meant to exclude other essential elements of your calling or limit the capacity of your service. God may intend for our ministry platform to be broader than these, and it may shift over time. We should be careful not to limit how God may use us and focus more on the direction of our calling rather than its details.

Another aspect of calling we should clarify is *duration*. As life changes and ministry shifts, we can be conflicted over our calling and our desire to remain faithful. While Scripture speaks of a vocational calling as a divine purpose for a lifetime (Jer. 1:5; Gal. 1:15), there are seasons in life when our ministry may take different forms. But these new roles do not require us to abandon our calling; they are, rather, opportunities for us to fulfill it in a different context. For instance, you may shift from serving as a student pastor to a senior pastor. Or, after years of serving as a pastor, you may transition to a role involved in training pastors while ministering as an interim for local congregations. Some may shift to a platform of denominational service that enables them to equip ministry leaders who multiply their investment into countless churches. And yet many ministry leaders occupy the same role throughout their years of service. The possibilities and platforms for ministry are endless, and so is our calling. Therefore, we must adopt a lifetime mindset, be faithful in our ministry opportunities, and shift with the seasonal changes as the Lord leads.

> The possibilities and platforms for ministry are endless, and so is our calling.

Commit without Conditions

Perhaps the greatest challenge we all face in wrestling with the call is coming to the final point of surrender. We know that when we "tap out," it changes everything. Our plans, our dreams, our goals, our passions, even our relationships, they ALL immediately fade into the background as God's purpose is given ultimate priority. But coming to that point and being truly willing to lay those things down isn't easy. Like parachuting from an airplane or launching off a high-ropes obstacle for the first time, stepping out and letting go is hard. It's scary and can even be painful. But once you jump, it is invigorating! It comes with freedom, hope, and a supernatural peace!

While a jumping comparison may be helpful, we also know that it doesn't quite compare. We're talking about the rest of your life! God's call deserves to be toiled over and carefully discerned before it can be fully embraced. The magnitude of surrendering to God's call is evident in several biblical examples of those God called to a specific ministry. As you prepare to commit without conditions to God's calling, their responses can provide some important reminders for you to consider.

While it may seem obvious, as you discern God's will on your life, *don't run from your calling*. No one plans to do this or dreams about growing up to "be like Jonah." But, when God's timing doesn't line up with our plans, when his calling isn't exactly what we had in mind, or when our preferences aren't fully considered, we often run the other way. When God called Jonah to go preach to Nineveh, he fled from God's presence and went the opposite direction (Jonah 1:1–3). Jonah's willingness to serve the Lord was contingent on God's will agreeing with his! But fleeing didn't free Jonah; it brought storms into his life (and to those around him!) that led him to the point of despair. Running from your calling invites God's gracious discipline that is never pleasant, but it is redemptive (Heb. 12:7–11). God rescued Jonah, and while he reluctantly obeyed, his heart never fully embraced God's call through willing surrender. Regardless of what God's plan for our lives requires or involves, we should never run from our calling.

Although you may not be tempted to run from God's calling, insecurity and feelings of inadequacy can bring hesitancy. But, as you wrestle with these understandable reservations, *don't resist your calling*. Resistance does not reflect stubbornness (like Jonah) but a delayed obedience driven by doubts. In Exodus 3–4, the Lord called Moses to put aside the shame and guilt of his previous failures in order to lead his people out of Egypt (Exod. 3:10). Moses responded with several questions and excuses that expressed his heart's reluctance. He ultimately pleaded with God, "Please, Lord, send someone else" (Exod. 4:13). But God responded to each of his questions with the reassurance of his plan and his presence. When Moses eventually surrendered, he not only led God's people to freedom, but he also obeyed with confidence and overcame every obstacle he originally feared and even greater ones he couldn't have imagined! Esther had a similar experience and initial response to God's call on her life. An evil plot to extinguish God's people was uncovered and defeated as she became a willing young lady who eventually embraced the reality that the Lord had set her apart "for such a time as this" (Esther 4:14).

Like Esther and Moses, it's understandable that we don't feel worthy to be used by God or capable of fulfilling his will for our lives. Previous failures can haunt us. The fear of how other people will respond can intimidate us. Our inabilities can make us doubt ourselves and even question God's wisdom to call us! But, as the familiar sayings remind us, "God doesn't call the qualified; he qualifies the called!" And "the only ability God is looking for is our availability!"

Sometimes God's plan doesn't line up with our time line. Maybe we want God to wait. Or, like Moses, we just want God to send someone else. But if you resist your call, God won't release you from your call. He desires to use you and is determined to use you! So by faith and with confidence in his faithfulness, we must come to the point of willing surrender and embrace Isaiah the prophet's response, "Here I am. Send me" (Isa. 6:8).

Running from and resisting God's call are struggles we must avoid or overcome. But there's one final caution you must remember as you embrace his call on your life: *don't resent your calling.* Resentment seeps into our hearts when we obey God's call out of some sense of spiritual obligation ("I've *got* to . . .") instead of grateful obedience ("I *get* to . . ."). Sadly, many ministry leaders serve with underlying bitterness and frustration that reflect this mindset. For some, they wish they had been called to do something else and never get over what they believe they had to sacrifice to go into ministry. Or maybe they believe they were somehow "forced" into ministry based on other people's expectations. Others are jealous of God's call on someone else's life and are convinced they'd be more satisfied if they could be in the other person's position. But it doesn't always come from jealousy or regret. Disappointment, discouragement, and defeat are part of ministry, and in those dark moments or seasons, we can begin to resent our calling.

The apostle Peter struggled with some of these things. After Jesus's death and resurrection, Peter went back to his previous occupation of fishing. He was disheartened and didn't know what to do next. But Jesus confronted Peter with the repeated question, "Do you love me?," and Peter became despondent. When Peter adamantly affirmed his love for him, Jesus proceeded to call him to "shepherd my sheep" (John 21:15–17). He then informed Peter that answering his call would result in his execution (vv. 18–19). Imagine the exasperation he would have felt! Peter's response was to immediately compare his calling to John's as he asked, "Lord, what about him?" (vv. 20–21). Jesus admonished Peter by explaining that his calling must be accepted without condition or comparison. Jesus's exhortation to Peter is the same for each of us: we are simply called by our Savior to "follow me" (vv. 19, 22). Embracing God's call frees you to enjoy the deep satisfaction that only comes from fulfilling his will, and it allows you to trust him to be the loving Father who always works for your good and his glory. Knowing this, we can commit to our calling without conditions.

Conclusion

In AD 1519, the Spanish Commander Hernán Cortés landed his fleet of ships on the shores of Veracruz (modern-day Mexico). As legend has it, Cortés was outmanned with only six hundred soldiers and ill equipped compared to the well-armored Aztec army who occupied the land they sought to conquer. But as his men disembarked, he ordered them to "burn the ships." Without their boats retreat was not an option. They would either win the war or die in defeat. History records that Cortés and his men fought for two years with vigor and resolve knowing that "giving up" was not an option. Eventually, they won the war and claimed the victory.

This well-known story illustrates an important mindset related to wrestling with our call. When we discern God's call to ministry on our lives, there are no other options. Our surrender requires us to "burn the ships" and not look back. We belong to him, and his purpose for our lives must prevail. Embracing our calling ultimately requires us to adopt the mindset the apostle Paul expressed as he tearfully left some of his closest friends in Ephesus to pursue the next steps of his calling. "I consider my life of no value to myself; my purpose is to finish my course and the ministry I received from the Lord Jesus, to testify to the gospel of God's grace" (Acts 20:24).

CHAPTER 2

Abiding in Christ

September 18, 2004 is a special day to me (Shane). It is my wedding day and the glorious day that I married way over my head. I thought I looked good because I wore a rented tuxedo, but when the double doors at the back of the sanctuary opened and I could see my bride, let me just say that she looked much, much better!

On this blessed day Kasi and I stood before God and our assembled witnesses to make a covenant to him and to each other. And on this day my identity completely changed. Sure, I still had the same name and the same DNA, but something else radically changed that day. I entered that church building as a single man but left as a husband.

This would be my new identity. I am not working to become a husband. I don't die, then go off to a distant place to become a husband. Nope! That very day, September 18, 2004, I became a husband. Now, for the last seventeen-plus years (at the time of this writing), I've been learning how to be who I already am—a husband!

And you should be proud of me because over the last seventeen years I've learned some things. For example, I've learned that there are fifteen pillows on our bed that I'm not allowed to sleep on. I've learned that any noise after 9:00 p.m., it's my job to figure what it is. I've also learned that I am significantly more handsome to my wife when I do the dishes. I've learned a lot of things, and for the rest of my earthly life, I'll be learning how to be who I already am.

That is exactly what it means to follow Jesus as a born-again (John 3:7) child of the Most High God. In the moment you were bought with the blood of Jesus, and the Holy Spirit came to live inside of you, your identity changed. Yes, you still have the same name and the same DNA, but something radically changed for you that day!

> You went from being spiritually lost to being spiritually found.
>
> You went from being a sinner separated from God to a saint who is one with God.
>
> You went from being spiritually dead to being spiritually alive.
>
> You went from being empty to being filled with the Holy Spirit.

> You went from being a broken person to a new creation in Christ.

> You went from being an orphan because of sin to being a child of God because of salvation.

Your identity changed in that moment. You're not working to become a child of God. You don't die and go somewhere else to become a child of God. You're a child of God right now, and for the rest of your life, you get to learn how to be who you already are—a child of God.

That is what discipleship and sanctification are. Moment by moment and day by day you learn what it means to live as a child of God, a follower of Jesus, a Christian. It's all about abiding in Christ for salvation and sanctification. Plus, serving in ministry and living on mission doesn't change any of that. The power you're going to need to effectively serve Jesus and his bride will ultimately come from abiding in him (John 15:4–5).

When Jesus bought you with his blood on the cross, you became a part of his bride—the church. You became one with him. This is what it means to abide in Christ. You're connected with him in a way that changes who you are, and he is giving you the power and sustenance to do what he is calling you to do.

Abide in Your Identity, Not Your Activity

Have you ever noticed the writing style of the apostle Paul? Nearly all of his letters are written in the same format. He starts with a greeting. Then he quickly moves into gospel truths. Paul talks about who God is. He writes about the work of Christ. Then he moves into how the gospel works in the lives of believers. Simply, this is who God is, this is what the gospel is, and this is who we are in Christ. Only then does he address how we must live because of these truths.

Basically, Paul says, this is who you *are*; now this is what you must *do*. He addresses our *identity* before he addresses our *activity*. You can see this clearly in the prison epistles—Ephesians, Philippians, Colossians, and Philemon.

Let's take a brief look at this progression in the book of Colossians.

Greeting: "To the saints in Christ at Colossae, who are faithful brothers and sisters. Grace to you and peace from God our Father" (Col. 1:2).

Who Jesus is: "He is the image of the invisible God, the first-born over all creation" (Col. 1:15). Then, on through verse 20 is an incredible description of Christ.

The work of the gospel: "Once you were alienated and hostile in your minds as expressed in your evil actions. But now he has reconciled you by his physical body through his death, to present you holy, faultless, and blameless before him" (Col. 1:21–22).

The identity change of the believer: "Therefore, as God's chosen ones, holy and dearly loved" (Col. 3:12).

Now, because of who you are, this is what you do: "Put on compassion, kindness, humility, gentleness, and patience, bearing with one another and forgiving one another if anyone has a grievance against another. Just as the Lord has forgiven you, so you are also to forgive. Above all, put on love, which is the perfect bond of unity" (Col. 3:12–14).

When we as believers truly grasp this truth, it is so refreshing. The gospel changes who we *are* before it changes what we *do*. The Holy Spirit will change your *identity*, then over time will begin to change your *activity*. It truly is a journey of learning how to be who you already are.

You must understand this and constantly remind yourself of this truth as a ministry leader. Your identity is in Christ and his work through the gospel. It is not in your leadership role or your work for the church. You must remember this because our natural tendencies will be to constantly stray away from this truth and find our worth in what we do for Jesus instead of in Jesus himself.

In ministry you also can't forget that we're in a war. This war is not against other people but against Satan and his army of demonic spirits (Eph. 6:12). Satan places a bull's-eye on those whom Christ has called into ministry and missions. One of the ways he will constantly attack you is through challenging your identity. This is exactly what he did to Jesus in the wilderness.

Toward the end of Matthew chapter 3, we see the beautiful account of John the Baptist baptizing Jesus. Can you imagine being John in that moment? Baptizing the Son of God! I still remember the first person I baptized. I was both excited beyond measure and equally nervous. If you've gotten to baptize someone already, you know the feeling. If you've yet to have that opportunity, I pray that soon you will. But can you imagine baptizing Jesus? We'd all be overwhelmed in that moment. Yet here is John the Baptist baptizing Jesus by immersion, and at that moment the Messiah comes up out of the water, there is an awesome display of the Trinity. God the

Son has been baptized, God the Holy Spirit descends on Him like a dove, then comes the voice of God the Father clearly identifying who Jesus is (Matt. 3:16–17).

The voice of the Father declares the identity of Jesus. Don't miss this truth. The declaration is for those witnessing this monumental event, but it is also an encouragement to Jesus. To be clear, Jesus knows who He is. However, it was a great moment of affirmation from the Father because the wilderness was coming and so was the enemy.

Moving into Matthew 4, Jesus is in the wilderness and has been fasting there for forty days. By this time he is physically hungry, thirsty, and exhausted. Then here comes Satan with an arsenal of temptations. On a side note, you need to realize this is the same strategy he uses against God-called leaders today; he comes to tempt when you are weak and exhausted. And before he tempts you with sinful activity, he will challenge your identity.

> If you abide in your Christ-given identity, then your activity for Christ will be healthy. However, if your identity is outside of Christ, then your activity for Christ will be unhealthy.

With Jesus there were temptations—food, testing God, and power. Each of these was preceded by the enemy trying to create doubt in Christ's identity. "Then the tempter approached him and said, 'If you are the Son of God, . . .'" (Matt. 4:3). "And said to him, "If you are the Son of God, . . ." (Matt. 4:6). "If you will fall down and worship me" (Matt. 4:9). Notice how Satan says, "If you are the Son of God," then calls Jesus to worship him, and yet Jesus is the only One worthy of worship. These are all attacks on the identity of Christ in an attempt to entice him toward sinful activity.

This a reality that everyone in ministry and leadership must understand. If you abide in your Christ-given identity, then your activity for Christ will be healthy. However, if your identity is outside of Christ, then your activity for Christ will be unhealthy. Who you *are* will determine what you *do*.

So, how does Jesus withstand this onslaught of temptations? First and foremost, he abides in his identity (Matt. 3:17). He knows who he is and knows that his Father is already pleased with him. Second, He abides in the Word of God, by constantly responding, "It is written" (Matt. 4:4, 7, 10).

All these same things are true for Christian leaders, ministers, and missionaries today. You must abide in the overflow of your identity as a child of God, abide in the truth that he is well pleased with you because of who you are in Christ, and abide constantly in God's Word.

Abide in the Overflow, Not the Flow That Is Over

As leaders, we must operate from the overflow and not the flow that has been over. Meaning we must live, serve, and lead from the overflow of abiding in Christ and avoid running the race of ministry on empty. Think of ministry like a cup full of water that is constantly being poured out. If nothing is being poured back into it, then it is only a matter of time before it is empty. This is exactly what happens at some point to nearly every Christian leader. Eventually, they will feel empty, exhausted, and burned out because they are constantly pouring into others but not being poured into themselves. And just like a car, we will go nowhere on empty.

However, let's even take this a step further. Instead, of pouring out, then being poured back into, what if we operated from a constant overflow of Christ's power, provision, and passion? Think of it now like a cup that water is being constantly poured into and it's overflowing and getting everything around it soaked. What if Christian leaders lived, served, and led in that way? When we abide in our identity in Christ, operate in our calling from Christ, and walk in intimacy with Christ in such a way that His love and power are overflowing out of us and affecting everything and everyone around us for His glory. This would truly change the world!

So, how do you do that? TIME! You have to spend time with the Lord. Overflow comes from intimacy. Spend time in the Word of God eating for yourself, not just preparing meals for others. The Bible can't just be a tool to write sermons and studies; it is the very bread we live by (Matt. 4:4). Often, leaders are attempting to feed others while starving themselves.

Also, prayer, listening, meditating on God's truth, silence and solitude, rest, reading books about Christian living and doctrine—basically, spending real time with your heavenly Father. Sadly, many of us are telling others about the God that we don't know very well ourselves, because we're not really spending much time with him ourselves.

Everyone loves to eat. Some love to eat so much that when they don't eat, they get angry. There is a word for this unfortunate phenomenon—hangry. When you don't feed your soul, inevitably your flesh will show its ugly face. Your soul can become hangry, too.

Typically, the progression will go like this: if you're away from God for a day or two, you know it. If that turns into a week or two, the people closest to you will know it. If it turns into a month or two, the people in your ministry will know it.

If it turns into years, sadly, everyone will probably know it because you'll most likely be burned out, empty, exhausted, and possibly completely out of ministry. As Michael Todd Wilson and Brad Hoffmann put it in their book *Preventing Ministry Failure,* "Nothing is more essential as ministers than our vibrant personal relationship with the One who both called us and sustains us. Without it, we have nothing to offer of any real value to anyone."[1]

> Sadly, many of us are telling others about the God that we don't know very well ourselves, because we're not really spending much time with him ourselves.

Once again the apostle Paul gives us this all-important model of abiding in identity and letting the activity operate from the overflow of that reality. In 2 Corinthians, he reminds the church of the gospel work in their life: "Therefore, if anyone is in Christ, he is a new creation; the old has passed away, and see, the new has come" (5:17). What great news he points people to! If you're a follower of Jesus, then you're a new creation. That is your identity. No longer defined by the old you or your old way of doing things. Then he continues to say, "Everything is from God, who has reconciled us to himself through Christ and has given us the ministry of reconciliation" (v. 18). Because you are a new creation in Christ and have been reconciled to God, he has given you a ministry.

This is a wonderful and freeing reality. Before the Lord ever called you to ministry or missions, before he ever gives you a title, church position, puts your name on a business card or website, before you're ever put on a stage or in a classroom, he just called you to know Jesus and to follow him. You will always be most effective when you are leading, ministering, serving, teaching, and discipling others when you're doing it out of the overflow of your own worship of Jesus and by abiding in him. Never, ever forget that.

CHAPTER 3

Loving the Scriptures

To be called to ministry means that we are called to be "set apart." Jesus prayed for all of his disciples to be *in* the world but not *of* the world (John 17:14–16). But because we've been set apart for the work of ministry, it's even more critical for us to be set apart from the world and its mindset. This is much easier read than done. Whether it's through people's social media stories, music that celebrates a particular lifestyle, or movies and shows that promote worldly pleasures and pursuits, our minds are constantly bombarded with our culture's views and values. Our hearts can quickly become flooded with toxic thoughts that influence what we desire and how we live. Gradually we can be deceived into pursuing the world's vanishing mirage of the ideal life that will always leave us empty and disappointed. This is exactly where I (Scott) found myself after graduating from college and becoming a successful accountant and business manager.

But God's Word tells us that we should "not be conformed" to the pattern of the world and its thinking. Instead, we are called to be "transformed by the renewing of [our] mind" so that we can properly discern God's "good, pleasing, and perfect will" (Rom. 12:2). When we read this biblical caution and challenge, somehow we can be convinced that pursuing God's plan is second-rate. Sure, we want to follow his will, but based on what the world is promoting, it seems like we're settling for less. This feeling can sometimes be hiding in our hearts and reveals our polluted perspective. And the only way to clarify our understanding is to catch a glimpse and become enamored with what the "good life" really looks like.

The book of Psalms begins with the picture and promise of the real "blessed" life. In Psalm 1 the author provides a contrast between an empty life that leads to ruin (vv. 1, 4–6) and the satisfied life that is righteous and rewarding (vv. 2–3, 6). The psalmist paints the picture of a strong tree that is grounded and growing, its leaf never withers, and it is planted by the water and produces desirable fruit. This tree represents the stable and satisfying life God desires for us. Perhaps the most important truth to notice is the source of strength and nourishment that produces this type of tree. The "flowing streams" represent the water of God's Word, and apart from its steady supply, the tree (and our lives) will wilt.

When we immerse ourselves in Scripture, having our minds and our hearts refreshed by its truth, we are assured that our lives and ministries will be fruitful and fulfilling. Therefore, we must plant our lives by the water of his Word to soak it in, saturate our heart, and squeeze it out as we minister to others in service to him.

Soak It In: Knowing the Word

Saturating our lives with Scripture begins with absorbing God's Word and soaking it in. While all believers must nourish their faith on the truth of God's Word, it's especially important for those of us who are called to ministry leadership. After the death of Moses, God anointed Joshua as the leader of his people. The Lord's primary charge to Joshua was to meditate on his Word continually and obey it completely (Josh. 1:8). This would not only ensure his success, but it would also assure him of God's presence and blessing. In the same way, our faithfulness and confidence in the Lord will be determined by our devotion and obedience to God's Word.

Our reliance on Scripture begins by recognizing it as the primary source for our *spiritual delight*. Whether you typically enjoy reading, soaking in God's Word is not like reading a novel, a biography, or a literary classic. The Bible is no ordinary book! It consists of sixty-six books written by forty different authors over a period of fifteen hundred years. Amazingly, all the writings are fully compatible, complementing one another without any contradiction. And because of the more than twenty-five thousand ancient manuscripts, it is the most authenticated text in history!

> Saturating our lives with Scripture begins with absorbing God's Word and soaking it in.

But the Bible is more than just those important facts. It is the Word of God. In other words, Scripture is the written expression of who and how God is. It is God speaking to us personally, revealing his mercy and grace, his power and majesty, and his love for you and me. As we marvel at his glory and rejoice in his goodness, the Bible floods our hearts with a supernatural gladness. When we consume it, Scripture becomes the delight and joy of our hearts (Jer. 15:16). It comforts us in affliction, cherishes God's blessings in our lives, provides wisdom, and celebrates the greatness of our God and King! Scripture gives the blueprint for building a truly satisfying life. It is the treasure map that leads to true riches in Christ, and it is the personal invitation that requests our presence to enjoy sweet fellowship with our Savior. Its value is immeasurable, and its worth is more than "an abundance of pure gold" (Ps. 19:10). No wonder the psalmist exclaimed, "How I love your instruction!" (Ps. 119:97).

In addition to delighting in the personal encounter, we can also delight in its divine nature and timeless truth. The broader story of Scripture reveals God's heart through the historical accounts of creation, sin and separation, the formation of his covenant people, his plan of redemption through the atoning death and resurrection of Jesus Christ, and his eternal glory that all believers will share with him. But the Bible is not just a summary of redemptive history. God continues to speak to us through what he has spoken (Rom. 15:4). His Word is alive and active, and he uses it to work in our lives (Heb. 4:12). In this way, it is powerful, penetrating, and personal.

As we acknowledge its unique nature, we must affirm several core convictions about Scripture that establish it as the foundation for our life and ministry. First, we believe the Bible is *inspired* (2 Tim. 3:16). In other words, God is the divine author of Scripture. Through his Spirit, God directed his chosen authors to record his sacred Word (2 Pet. 1:20–21). Divine inspiration means that every piece, part, and passage are significant and eternal (Matt. 5:18; 1 Pet. 1:23–25). Additionally, we believe that God's Word is *inerrant,* or "without error." Scripture is wholly and completely true in every word. It is perfect and pure as it reflects the character of God (Ps. 19:7–9). Finally, we believe the Bible is *infallible.* This means it is not only true but also trustworthy. It won't misguide or mislead you in any way. It is right and reliable since God "cannot lie" (Titus 1:2), and "the word of the LORD proves true" (Ps. 18:30 ESV). These three core convictions also mean that the Bible functions as God's Word in its authority and sufficiency. Therefore, we must build our lives and ministries on the truth of Scripture. Because of its divine nature and infinite value, we must treasure and trust the Bible as our source of spiritual delight.

Not only is it the source of our spiritual delight, but God's Word is also the source of our *spiritual development.* Scripture is essential for every aspect of our spiritual life. While we may live in a world with unlimited options, when it comes to our relationship with the Lord, there is no substitute for God's Word. It is the source of our salvation as it reveals the truth of God's holiness, man's sinfulness, and Christ's forgiveness. The "sacred Scriptures" provide the "wisdom for salvation through faith in Christ Jesus" (2 Tim. 3:15). God works through the power of his Word to grant us new life and to be "born again" (1 Pet. 1:23; James 1:18).

The Bible is not only God's chosen means for our spiritual birth, but it is also his chosen means for our spiritual growth. Just as our bodies require physical nutrition, our spiritual nourishment comes from a steady consumption of God's Word (Matt. 4:4). Therefore, "like newborn infants" you should "desire the pure milk of the word, so that by it you may grow up into your salvation" (1 Pet. 2:2). As we mature, we must grow in our knowledge and understanding of the Word so that we may be "complete, equipped for every good work" (2 Tim. 3:16–17). A growing hunger for God's Word develops our spiritual discernment (Heb. 5:12–14). Ultimately, the Lord sanctifies us and makes us more like Jesus through his divine truth (John 17:17).

> Scripture is essential for every aspect of our spiritual life.

To be spiritually dependent on the Lord and his Word for our development means everything we do must be informed and infused with Scripture. The Bible has the power to supernaturally transform our hearts as we apply it to the various aspects of our life and ministry. As we submit ourselves to his Word, it encourages our walk with the Lord (Col. 2:6–7), enhances our worship of the Lord (Col. 3:16), enables us to work for the Lord (Col. 3:23), and equips us to witness for the Lord (Col. 4:5–6). As we soak it in, we must allow Scripture to saturate every area of our lives.

The Bible is the source of our spiritual delight and development and is also the source of our *spiritual defense*. As we grow in Christ, we must be armed with the truth of God's Word to guard ourselves against our sinful desires and our spiritual adversary. Some of the greatest struggles we will face in life and ministry will emerge from our own heart. Pride, lust, jealousy, selfish ambition, anger, discouragement, apathy, and self-righteousness are all sinful desires that we must actively combat by taking in God's Word (Ps. 119:9–11). The Bible helps us identify willful and unintentional sin in our lives, even our "hidden faults" (Ps. 19:11–13). When we submit ourselves to Scripture, it becomes a mirror that reveals and addresses our spiritual blemishes (James 1:22–25). Scripture even judges the thoughts and intentions of our inner being. God uses it like a scalpel to perform sanctifying surgery on our hearts (Heb. 4:12).

Along with being God's sanctifying scalpel, the Bible is also God's piercing sword that equips us to combat the enemy. In the spiritual war against Satan and the forces of darkness, we must "put on the full armor of God," including "the sword of the Spirit—which is the word of God" (Eph. 6:10–17). When Jesus was tempted, he resisted Satan by repeatedly wielding Scripture as his weapon (Matt. 4:1–11). God's Word has the power to disarm and defeat the enemy.

In order to arm ourselves with the sword of the Spirit, we must learn to navigate the Scriptures and be familiar with verses and passages that address areas of struggle in our life and ministry. Memorizing specific verses and meditating on them regularly will help us guard our hearts against temptation and defend ourselves in moments of personal battle. Whether it is our spiritual desires or the spiritual enemy, Scripture is our source of spiritual defense.

Saturate Your Heart: *Growing in the Word*

While knowing God's Word is a foundational part of our spiritual progress, growing in God's Word is essential for us to fulfill our spiritual purpose. Biblical teaching is a crucial aspect of any vocational call to ministry. While not everyone is called to be a pastor who is charged to "preach the word" (2 Tim. 4:2) and must be "able to teach" (1 Tim. 3:2), all those who serve the Lord and minister to others must be equipped to share the truth of Scripture (Col. 3:16; 1 Tim. 4:13). Your teaching may involve personal mentoring or small-group leadership rather than a stage in a sanctuary. Still, regardless of the size of your platform, the size of the task is huge. In fact, it can seem overwhelming. But when we love the Scriptures, we will saturate our hearts with a deep and personal knowledge of God's Word that prepares us to faithfully teach it in whatever context he calls us to serve. Our heart saturation is essential and benefits us in three primary ways.

The main reason we must saturate our hearts with God's Word is because it provides *deeper study.* Our motivation for studying the Bible should not be because we have a message to prepare. We should come to God's Word with a desire for a personal encounter with the Lord that will transform our hearts. As a result, we can teach from the overflow of what God has taught us. We don't study because we have to teach; we teach because we have studied. This prioritized sequence is crucial, and we must be

> We don't study because we have to teach; we teach because we have studied.

careful to maintain it. Our hearts must be devoted to studying and obeying God's Word. This will equip us to teach his truth to his people (Ezra 7:10).

This raises a common and important question for those who are called to ministry: Can our devotional study be used as teaching preparation? Some ministry leaders draw a sharp line of distinction that forbids any overlap between the two while others will intentionally spend their personal devotion time praying through and meditating on their teaching passage. Both perspectives have value, and each can be maintained through personal and prayerful balance. We can't substitute devotional reading and reflection for the rigorous study of the text that our teaching should require. But we also need to preserve our intimacy with Christ and not simply spend time analyzing a passage that neglects our own spiritual nourishment. In other words, if the only time you read the Bible is because you are preparing to teach, then you are simply peddling a product you don't own and can't personally endorse. Saturating our hearts with Scripture through both aspects of study provides mutual benefits for our life and ministry.

> If the only time you read the Bible is because you are preparing to teach, then you are simply peddling a product you don't own and can't personally endorse.

Another reason we must saturate our hearts is because those who are called to teach the Bible are held to *a higher standard* (James 3:1). This may sound intimidating, but it reinforces how essential it is for us to be saturated with God's Word. Some of the "stricter judgment" involves an elevated scrutiny as our lives are evaluated by others based on the words we teach. Any inconsistency between what we are teaching and how we are living will be magnified by our role as teachers. More importantly, we are held to a higher standard by the Lord because of the spiritual influence we have on others as teachers of his Word.

Our accountability before the Lord is ultimately determined by how faithfully we handle the Scriptures. As the apostle Paul challenged his spiritual protégé, Timothy, "Be diligent to present yourself to God as one approved, a worker who doesn't need to be ashamed, correctly teaching the word of truth" (2 Tim. 2:15). This verse teaches us that we can be "approved" by God and don't have to be "ashamed" if we are "correctly teaching" his Word. But this requires us to "be diligent" in our study of Scripture to ensure our faithfulness to his Word as well as our calling.

In addition to a deeper study and higher standard, a saturated heart is also necessary because it provides us *a wider scope.* Too many people, even in ministry, have a limited understanding of the Bible. This is evidenced by a frequent focus on familiar passages and recurring truths. While foundational aspects of Scripture should be reinforced, a love for the Scriptures opens our hearts to appreciate the comprehensive beauty and depth of God's Word. We should be committed to teaching the whole counsel of God (Acts 20:27) as we magnify Christ as the supreme subject of all the Scriptures (Luke 24:27).

This requires us to expand our personal study beyond the passages that are comfortable and customary. But, as you continue to saturate your heart with Scripture through personal study, you will find that your teaching preparation will be enhanced and become more efficient. Your increasing familiarity with the Bible will allow you to identify supplemental passages, cross-references, and redemptive themes that reinforce the truth of the text you will be teaching. This not only provides a level of comfort and confidence for you as a teacher, but it will also help your listeners appreciate the rich consistency of the Scriptures.

Because of our calling and our responsibility to teach God's Word, saturating your heart with Scripture is essential. It ultimately enhances our intimacy with Christ through deeper study, equips us to be faithful to God's higher standard, and expands our love for the Scriptures through a wider scope that treasures all of his Word.

Squeeze It Out: *Sowing the Word*

As we devote ourselves to knowing and growing in God's Word, our calling also involves sowing his Word. As spiritual seeds, the truth of God's Word is meant to be planted into the hearts of others so that it will take root and bear fruit for God's glory (James 1:21). Our desire is to see people become like the tree planted by the water that continues to be nourished and refreshed by its life-giving power (Ps. 1:3). As we soak in God's Word, we must squeeze it out into the lives of others.

In leading and serving our people, one of the most difficult things to learn is how to minister to them in various situations. We often find ourselves at a loss for words as we attempt to console people in moments of despair. We may not know what to say when someone is struggling or how to answer their questions when they are spiritually confused. There may be times when we need to lovingly confront our people and challenge them in their walk with the Lord. These scenarios are intimidating, but in those moments, our love for the Bible can equip us to serve them well.

When we saturate our hearts with Scripture, we will have *a word to encourage God's people.* Whether it's a moment of crisis or an everyday challenge, it is easy for people to become discouraged. But God's Word can provide them with joy, hope, and peace as they struggle through a difficult situation or extended season of hardship. In order to minister to them, we must be equipped with verses or passages of Scripture that can meet them where they are. This doesn't mean that we want to preach to struggling people during their hurt and heartache. We simply want to be ready with a verse to share with them as we hold their hand to pray or to send to them as we reach out to encourage them. Preparing in advance by identifying certain verses or passages that speak to various struggles and scenarios can be helpful. But the greatest preparation will come through our ongoing devotion to God's Word.

As we encourage God's people with his Word, it's not always related to difficulty or pain. Often our encouragement will be more of an exhortation that propels them forward in their faith. The Bible regularly instructs ministry leaders to compel God's people to "excel still more" (1 Thess. 4:1, 10 NASB1995). Calling people to deeper intimacy with Christ and to faithfully live for him requires us to challenge them with an appeal and instruction that is thoroughly biblical. In other words, as we encourage our people to grow in the Lord, it won't be accomplished by our passion and enthusiasm. God's

Word must be the authoritative voice, the motivating impulse, and the practical standard that stimulates and guides their obedience. Our ability to properly encourage and exhort God's people will be greatly enhanced by our own growth in God's Word.

In addition to offering encouragement, when our hearts are saturated with Scripture, we will also have *a word to equip God's people*. In the previous section, we saw how this relates to our ministry responsibility of teaching those who are under our care. But beyond our typical discipleship efforts, many times our people will look to us for explanations and answers to life's most challenging questions. They may be theological or practical. Whether they are trying to make the right decision or wrestling through a deep truth that is difficult to understand, we want to be careful that we don't simply offer up our opinions. We could set them up to fail or be disappointed. We can easily offer advice that misleads them or provide answers that confuse them. While they may or may not hold inadequate answers against us, it can undermine their faith as they often associate our counsel with the reliability of God's Word.

It is so critical for us to point our people to what the Bible says about an issue or to suggest Scriptures that provide the wisdom they need in making important decisions. This requires us to know God's Word through diligent study so that we can faithfully lead them. While no one can be prepared for every question, we should commit to continually growing in our biblical knowledge so that we can help them navigate God's Word and discern its truth together.

When God uses Scripture to transform our lives, he is simultaneously equipping us to minister to others through the power of his

Word. As you fulfill his calling and foster your love for Scripture by soaking it in and saturating your heart, the Lord will prepare you to squeeze it out into the lives of his people as you water the seed of God's Word from the overflow of your own life!

Conclusion

At the end of the Sermon on the Mount, Jesus summarized the significance of loving and obeying God's Word by telling a parable about two builders (Matt. 7:24–27). By way of comparison, both of them heard his word and both experienced difficult storms in their lives. By contrast, only one of them established God's truth as the sure and secure foundation of his life by submitting to his word in obedience. The other disregarded the truth he heard and built his life on the shifting sand of his own earthly wisdom. The difference was only realized when they both were "pounded" by the same blowing winds and battering waves of life. The storm resulted in the devastation and destruction for the foolish builder as his life "collapsed with a great crash." But the life of the wise builder, founded on the rock of God's truth, proved to be a stable fortress that weathered the rampage and stood as a testament to the truth and reliability of the word.

The parable Jesus told is certainly true for all believers. Everyone will choose to build their lives on one of the two foundations, the wisdom of his Word or the wisdom of this world. But for those of us who are called to ministry, the truth of this parable is even more profound for multiple reasons. One reason is because the storms and difficulties of ministry can be more intense and more frequent than the common storms of life. The foundation of our lives will be repeatedly tested, and the result, our catastrophic collapse or our fortitude by faith, will be revealed. As ministry leaders, how we respond will either undermine or fortify the faith of God's people.

All of this means that ultimately our success in ministry is predicated on the Scriptures. As we soak it in as the source of our spiritual development and defense and saturate our hearts through careful study and consistent devotion, we can squeeze it out to encourage and equip God's people through its overflow from our lives.

> Everyone will choose to build their lives on one of the two foundations, the wisdom of his Word or the wisdom of this world.

CHAPTER 4

Being Men and Women of Prayer

It was early 2003, I (Shane) wasn't married yet, but there was this blonde-haired, green-eyed girl that I was interested in. The current status of our relationship at that time was "we were talking." Which, back in the days of DVDs and iPods, that is how you'd described the process in a relationship journey right before being officially boyfriend and girlfriend, but we were definitely beyond the stage of just "liking" each other.

In my hands constantly was this little black Nokia phone with a plastic Miami Dolphins phone case on it. I primarily used that phone for two things—playing Snake (the only game on there) and talking to this girl. Every day I couldn't wait to call her or for her to call me. We'd talk about everything—future goals, dreams, what God had taught us that day, or more ordinary things like daily events or funny stories. More than anything I just loved her presence and hearing her voice. I wanted to know everything there was to know about her. I enjoyed talking to her so much that there were multiple months of multiple-hundred-dollar cell phone bills because I went well over my allotted monthly minutes. This obviously was before the glorious days of unlimited talk and text, but that is another conversation for a different day.

The point is that I had fallen in love with this girl and couldn't imagine going one single day without spending time with her, talking to her, listening to her, and just thinking about her. Fast-forward, this blonde-haired, green-eyed girl is now my wife, and I am more in love with her now than I was then. Over the years and through many life experiences, our relationship has grown, matured, and deepened. And I still deeply enjoy spending time with her, talking to her, listening to her, and sometimes just sitting with her and saying nothing at all. After all, it's her presence I desire the most. I want to be wherever she is.

This should be even more so with our great God. Our top desire as followers of Jesus Christ should be to constantly be in his presence. Wherever our Lord is, that is where we should want to be, to know him more and more every day, to listen to him, to talk to him, to think about him, and maybe sometimes to sit silently with him. Because we love him above all things, we want to know everything about him and to be with him as much as possible. In fact, we should dread any day this doesn't happen because we desire to be in his presence so deeply. His proximity is our passion. You can feel the same desire in the words of Psalm 42, "As a deer longs for flowing streams, so I long for you, God. I thirst for God, the living God. When can I come and appear before God?" (vv. 1–2).

Ultimately, this is what prayer is—time well spent in the presence of our great God, who also happens to be the most famous One of all and the Creator of the universe. What a great privilege this is! Prayer shouldn't be a burden or a task to check off a daily list. It is simply talking to, listening for, thinking about, and spending time with the One who loves us so much that he paid the ultimate sacrifice so that we could do this very thing.

However, if we were to be honest, this is probably the area where we fail the most as leaders. When we're not being men and women of prayer, it should feel as abnormal as being deeply in love with someone and never spending time with them—talking, listening, sitting in silence, or even thinking about them. If we don't spend time with someone or communicate with them, can we really say we love them? Does it make it any better if we have the desire but practically are too busy to be around them? Would we see that as healthy? Of course not! Then why do we approach prayer and communion with God so differently?

Maybe it has to do with some of our misconceptions when it comes to prayer. Before we dive into the depths of what prayer is, let's briefly step into the shallow end of what prayer is not. Prayer is not clasping your hands together with eyes closed, shouting at God in King James English. Prayer is not only "saying grace" over chicken wings and fries. Prayer isn't a transition in the corporate worship service between the third song and the preaching so that the musicians can put their guitars down and exit the stage. Prayer isn't even a public theological discourse in a crowd so everyone can hear how smart and well read you are.

Prayer is a lifestyle. It's our oxygen for life and ministry, our lifeline in spiritual warfare, and our connector to the greatest power source there is—God himself. Prayer is acknowledging the God who is with you. And while you follow him, it's an incredible opportunity and privilege getting to know him.

Prayer Is a Lifestyle

There is an old story of two college roommates who decided they wanted to start the new school year off right by praying together at the end of every day before heading off to their separate rooms at night. The first day of school starts, at about ten o'clock that night, and one roommate said to the other, "It's time to pray. I'll start." This first college student prayed for over thirty minutes using big fancy theological words and phrases. He prayed for any and everything imaginable—from thanking God for his Chick-fil-A lunch to the missionaries in Africa. Then finally closing out with a hearty "Amen!" Now came the turn of the second college student, who simply prayed, "Father, I had a great day with you. Thank you for everything you did, and thank you for who You are. I love You. Talk to you in the morning."

The first roommate was visibly frustrated and said in a snarky tone, "If you're not going to take this seriously, then we just won't do it! I've prayed this lengthy and ornate prayer, and all you prayed was a good-night sentiment." To which the second student humbly and lovingly replied, "Hey, I've been talking to my Father all day long, so all that was left to say was good night."

This story is an example of what prayer should look like for the follower of Jesus. It's just an ongoing relationship and conversation. Sometimes you're talking. At other times he is talking. Sometimes you're just enjoying each other's company in silence. And always your love and knowledge of him is growing.

The apostle Paul said, "Pray constantly" (1 Thess. 5:17). Prayer for the Christian is not a sporadic occurrence; it is a lifestyle. For men and women called to ministry, this can't just be one aspect of your ministry; this literally is your life and ministry. When God saves you and calls you, it becomes an ongoing relationship and conversation for the rest of your life here on earth, until he calls you home; then it will continue in heaven for all eternity.

Prayer was a lifestyle of Jesus as well. When you read the four Gospels, the most common habit of Jesus wasn't healing, preaching, walking on water, or even serving others. Yes, he did those things. But the practice of Jesus that is described more than any other was of him praying. The Bible speaks continually about Jesus praying. It was his lifestyle to speak continually to his Father. He prayed in public, in private, early in the morning, while ministering and healing, and while sweating drops of blood in the garden of Gethsemane. In fact, it seems as though everything he did in ministry—serving, leading, discipling, preaching, and ministering—were all from the overflow of his prayer ministry. It must be the same for us.

As those called to serve God and his people and to lead the church, we must be a praying people. In the Scriptures, prayer is described as the chief characteristic of the church. Look at what the

Lord says through his prophet Isaiah: "I will bring them to my holy mountain and let them rejoice in my *house of prayer*. Their burnt offerings and sacrifices will be acceptable on my altar, for my house will be called a *house of prayer* for all nations" (Isa. 56:7, emphasis added). Notice it doesn't say a "house of good music," a "house of dynamic preaching," a "house of beautiful décor," or even a "house with great ministries." The Bible describes the church as a "house of prayer." The number one descriptor of every church should be prayer.

Sadly, prayer in most churches is at the bottom of the priority list. We'd never say that, but it is what our practice shows. It's a five-minute prayer after going over a church prayer request sheet for forty-five minutes, or it's the transition between songs in the church's "run of show" for the worship service. Prayer isn't a tack-on at the end of a service or a transition in the middle of one. Prayer is a lifestyle for the believer and for the church.

However, as a leader, the ministry you're leading will never pray more than you do. You have to set the tone. If you want to lead a praying people, you must be a praying leader. Can you say that you're a person of prayer? Would others describe you that way? Do you see and live prayer out in a way that it is an ongoing relationship and conversation with you and your heavenly Father? What changes need to be made? Start the conversation right now if you must.

> The number one descriptor of every church should be prayer.

Prayer Is Your Oxygen

Simply put, we all make time to breathe. You never hear anyone say, "I'm just too busy to breathe. I really love oxygen, but I just don't have time for it." We make time to breathe because we know without oxygen we won't survive. In the Christian life and in ministry, we must view prayer in the same light. Without it we won't survive. It is our fuel for everything, our lifeblood, our lifeline. J. Oswald Sanders, in his classic book *Spiritual Leadership*, said, "Prayer is indeed the Christian's vital breath and native air."[1] Prayer is our spiritual oxygen, and just as oxygen is vital to our natural life, so prayer is vital to our spiritual life.

The Christian leader will always be able to use the excuse of being too busy, stretched too thin with responsibilities, and feeling too tired. However, this is even more reason why we must be men and women of prayer. Sanders also quoted the great reformer Martin Luther as saying on a particular day that he had a full workload: "Work, work from early till late. In fact, I have so much to do that I shall spend the first three hours in prayer."[2]

We get robbed of precious opportunities for prayer because we are distracted by noise and busyness. John Mark Comer, in his book *The Ruthless Elimination of Hurry*, writes about the moments of boredom we used to have before the constant distraction in our hands—the smartphone. There used to be moments while waiting to get your oil changed, sitting at the doctor's office, or standing in line at the coffee shop that would provide moments of boredom where we had no social media to feverishly scroll through. Comer said, "All those little moments of boredom were potential portals of prayer. Little moments throughout our days to wake up to the reality of God all around us."[3] The busier we are, and the greater the demands on our life and ministry, the more intentional we have to be in prayer. You must be intentional to have moments throughout the day when you remove distractions and focus in on God. Comer also said, "The noise of the modern world makes us deaf to the voice of God, drowning out the one input we most need."[4] If Jesus needed moments every day when he removed himself from busyness and distractions to focus on prayer for living and ministry, how much more do we need it?

Also, all the great leaders in the Bible were great at prayer. Highly effective Christian leaders understand that they will get nowhere in impacting eternity, kingdom building, and battling in spiritual warfare if they're not a praying people. When you read biographies of godly leaders, who the Lord used in extraordinary and unique ways, there was always one thing they all had in common: they were men and women of prayer.

I (Shane) live in Texas. That is the capital state for pickup trucks. Driving a truck is almost like a rite of passage. And not only for men—many women drive trucks. In fact, a popular bumper sticker plays off the old Trix cereal commercial by saying, "Silly boys, trucks are for girls!" However, the point is, I can have a beautiful black Ford F350 truck with lots of chrome, big tires, and a lift kit to make it even bigger. However, if I don't have fuel to put in it, it's not going anywhere. It may look pretty, but it basically turns into a large and expensive paperweight with no gas. It can be the same way in ministry. A ministry can be big and pretty, but if there is no fuel, it's not going anywhere in making a real kingdom impact. You can grow a crowd by human effort, but you can only grow a ministry by the power of God.

Remember, living the Christian life and serving in ministry is not a profession; it is a battle. It is spiritual warfare. Paul wrote, "For our struggle is not against flesh and blood, but against the rulers, against the authorities, against the cosmic powers of this darkness, against evil, spiritual forces in the heavens" (Eph. 6:12). If we're in a battle against spiritual things, we will desperately need the Spirit. To connect, grow, and be empowered by the Spirit has to come through a lifestyle of regular communion with him through prayer. Prayer is the fuel and oxygen for everything. It is also our connector to the power source, God himself.

Prayer Is the Power Cord

While I write this book, there is a lamp that is lighting up the desk. The lamp provides light in the darkness. It is a great help, but it is not a power source in and of itself. A lamp was created to light up a room. That is its purpose. However, it can't accomplish its purpose all by itself. For the lamp to fulfill its purpose and work the way it was created to work, it has to be plugged into a power source. So there is a power cord connected to the lamp that can be plugged into a power source that gives it the power to shine brightly and accomplish its purpose.

Our purpose for being created is to know God and to make him known. The calling on our life as a follower of Jesus is to be a light to the world (Matt. 5:14–16). For us to shine brightly in the world, and as leaders to equip others to do the same, we must be connected to a power source that actually shines through us. God is that power source, and the power cord is prayer.

Prayer must be seen as the highest of priorities because it is your connection to God. In ministry, without prayer you can do nothing good for God. No matter how great your intentions are, your work habits are, or how awesome your talents are. Jesus said of himself, "You can do nothing without me" (John 15:5).

> Our purpose for being created is to know God and to make him known.

A. C. Dixon said, "When we depend upon organizations, we get what organizations can do; when we depend upon education, we get what education can do; when we depend upon man, we get what man can do; but when we depend upon prayer, we get what God can do."[5] That should be our heart's desire as followers of Jesus and as those called to lead and shepherd his church. May we have this unction to want what only God can do. If everything in your life and ministry can be explained by your power and your efforts, you have to ask yourself, "Where is God in all of this?" May there be markers throughout your life and ministry that you look at and say, "This can only be explained by the power of God alone." And that can only happen when you're connected to the power source through prayer. Prayerlessness equals powerlessness in ministry.

Andrew Murray once said, "The sin of prayerlessness is one of the deepest roots of evil."[6] The Creator of the universe has invited us to spend time with him, to talk to him, and to learn from him. How incredibly arrogant do we have to be to think we don't need that?

When we're not praying, we're d
God. In a sense, we're saying, "G
I can handle being a Christian, a
a minister without you." Of cour
called to ministry would ever ve
that is practically what we're sayi
and women of prayer. Praying is
ing, "God, I desperately need you
do I want to. God, do what only
with you and to get to know you

The wonderful truth is, the I
time with you. He wants to work
to reveal himself to you and show
without spending time with him.
and tell you great and incompre
(Jer. 33:3).

CHAPTER 5

Being Soul Winners

There was about a year time gap between the moment I (Shane) started praying about going to Bible college and the actual time I moved to Dallas, Texas, to start the first semester. I was working in a warehouse and made quick friends with a guy named Brandon. Our workstations were right next to each other, and for the entire year we'd eat lunch and take breaks together. I was a brand-new Christian at the time, and in my own estimation was "on fire for Jesus." My wardrobe on most days would consist of jeans, sneakers, and some sort of Christian T-shirt. Also, most of the time I had worship music playing in my work area, or DC Talk's *Jesus Freak*. So, in my mind, I thought I was living on mission and being a soul winner because I had Christian swag on and was listening to Jesus music. However, the problem was that I never opened my mouth to tell Brandon about Jesus.

For an entire year, I had plenty to say about things that didn't really matter—sports, movies, and hobbies. But I had nothing to say about the only thing that truly mattered—the gospel. Toward the end of that year, Brandon came to work on a Monday morning with a big grin on his face. It was 8:00 a.m., and the first thing he said to me was, "Shane, aren't you a Christian?" (Isn't it sad that he had to ask?) I replied, "Yeah, man. I am. What's up?" He continued to tell me that he went to church the day before to watch his nephew get baptized, heard the gospel preached, and was given a clear invitation. Then he said, "Shane! I am now a Christian too! Yesterday I surrendered my life to Jesus!"

Oh, wow! I was ecstatic! I gave him a big hug while saying, "Dude! That's so awesome. I'm so excited for you! That means we are brothers in Christ now. You have to put up with me for all eternity!" Then I went to give him another hug, and he shoved me back. His demeanor changed into something serious. The smile was now disappearing as he began saying, "Shane, you know what else I heard yesterday? I heard that if you spend your whole life not knowing Jesus, and you're never born again, then die that way, you will end up in an eternity separated from all the goodness of God in a literal place called hell." Then he sternly said, "Do you believe that?" A knot immediately formed in my stomach, and a lump swelled in my throat as I muttered, "Yeah, man. I believe the Bible, and I believe it teaches that." I'll never, ever forget his next question. It's burned into my memory bank. With tears now streaming down this grown man's face, he says, "Did you not care enough about me to tell me that?"

What do you say to that? How do you reply? Everything we have to offer as excuses in those moments sounds extremely selfish. "I didn't want you to think I'm weird." "I didn't want you to get mad at me." "I was afraid you'd treat me like an outcast." "I didn't know what to say, so I didn't say anything." If we're honest, we mainly make the lack of our soul-winning efforts and personal evangelism about us—our convenience, our comfort, and our lack of confidence.

So, as followers of Jesus, we must ask ourselves daily, "Do we believe heaven and hell are real? Do we believe the gospel is for everyone? Do we believe it's our job to share? Do we even care if the people around us are spiritually lost?"

I wish I could say that it gets easier to be a soul winner when you're in ministry. However, it doesn't. Personal evangelism is never something you just accidently become effective at. You have to work at it. That's why Paul told young Timothy, "But as for you, exercise self-control in everything, endure hardship, do the work of an evangelist, fulfill your ministry" (2 Tim. 4:5).

Soul winning is also something you never stumble into; you must be intentional. There has to be an on-purpose and on-mission intentionality to being a soul winner yourself and a desire to duplicate it in others. So here are some practical ways to be intentional about being a soul winner and how to disciple others to do the same.

Cover Your Life in Prayer

Prayer is the fuel for every aspect of the Christian life, including evangelism. That's why a whole chapter in this book is dedicated to being men and women of prayer. Evangelism comes from two Greek words: *euaggelion*, which means "a good message, or gospel," and *euaggelizo*, which means "to announce, declare, bring, or preach this good news." The act of evangelism is a work of declaring the goodness of God to a world that desperately needs him. It's impossible to do the work of God effectively without God being at the center of that work. Prayer in evangelism is realizing and acting on the truth that nothing can be done without him. Lord, we desperately need you to do what only you can do—win souls.

There are a few rare supernatural stories that I've heard missionaries share about people coming to know Jesus through dreams or visions before the intentional work of the gospel was brought by believers to unreached people groups. However, most people who surrender their lives to Jesus for salvation do so because of the direct result of being prayed for by Christians, who were deeply burdened for them. In fact, you're most likely the result of loved ones praying for you to know Jesus, love Jesus, and follow Jesus in obedience to the calling he has placed on your life.

If you're going to be a soul winner, you must be a prayer warrior. Pray for spiritually lost people by name. Pray for a spiritual awakening in your circle of influence, in your city, in your nation, and in other nations. Pray for gospel opportunities in your daily life to point people to Jesus. Then pray for yourself. Pray and ask the Lord for spiritual eyes to see the opportunities he is providing. Then ask him for obedience, faith, and confidence to walk through those doors of gospel opportunities when he opens them. If you pray for God to provide opportunities for the gospel to be proclaimed, he will certainly answer that prayer. You must be ready when he does.

Evangelism birthed out of prayer will be fruitful, but evangelism without prayer will be largely ineffective. Paul said, "Rejoice in hope; be patient in affliction; be persistent in prayer" (Rom. 12:12).

Conviction over Convenience

Evangelism isn't a discipline or gifting for a few super-Christians; it is a calling for every believer. The purpose of every Christian is to know him and to make him known. It must be the conviction of your life, and most of the time it won't be convenient. If you're waiting for a convenient time to share the gospel with people, then you'll be waiting until Jesus comes back. Evangelism is about conviction, not convenience.

This doesn't stop once you're in ministry and a leader in the church. You may be thinking, *Duh. Do you even need to say that?* Unfortunately, the answer is yes, we do. As crazy as it sounds, some pastors, church staff, and ministry leaders think their main job is to preach, lead, and minister to Christians. They rarely focus on the spiritually lost people outside the church walls who desperately need the hope of Christ. Because of this sobering reality, Mark Dever says, "I generally know, when someone goes into the ministry because they like to work only with Christians and to do church things, that this person probably isn't called."[1] In that same vein, Dave Harvey, in his great little book *Am I Called?*, says, "God sent His Son to us. God sends pastors into the world. If you don't want to reach people with the gospel, you're probably not called to be a pastor. Pastors do the work of evangelism."[2]

Yes, those called to ministry are to lead, serve, and disciple believers. But we cannot neglect the work of evangelism. Paul told Timothy (who, was a pastor) to "do the work of an evangelist" (2 Tim. 4:5). In ministry, you'll mainly be around people who already know Jesus. Therefore, it takes intentionality to be around unbelievers, to invest in them, and to share the gospel with them. It's not easy or convenient by any means. It takes work. It takes conviction.

> For evangelism to be a conviction of a ministry, it must be a conviction of its leaders.

Being a soul winner should be an expectation of every believer. As a leader, you must model this for those you're discipling. People in your ministry will never do what you're not doing yourself. You create the standard. You set the example. For evangelism to be a conviction of a ministry, it must be a conviction of its leaders. Paul was able to tell the Corinthians with a clear conscience, "Imitate me as I also imitate Christ" (1 Cor. 11:1). When it comes to being soul winners, are you able to tell others with a clear conscience that they can imitate your conviction?

Coach Yourself and Others in the Gospel

One of the biggest reasons we don't share the gospel with people is because of fear. Even as leaders, sharing the gospel outside the walls of the church building can be intimidating. When people are at church, that is our turf. We have home-field advantage, so we're often not as afraid to share the gospel. After all, that's why they are there. They've come to hear about Jesus, and we're always ready to tell them.

However, away from the church building, we can lose our comfort and confidence. We're not as bold at the ball field, family gathering, or coffee shop. We'll talk about anything and everything while staying silent about the most important thing—the gospel. Pastors Jimmy Scroggins and Steve Wright point out a sobering reality when the say, "We can talk about sports, weather, clothes, shoes, movies, and TV shows. We're even willing to debate the nuance of politics, the intricacies of health issues, or the complexities of national economic matters. However, when it comes to bringing up the simple gospel, we shy away."[3]

In those public settings, people did not come to us; we've gone to them. So, we feel like we're on their turf. It feels like an "away game." We feel like we've lost the home-field advantage, so we get nervous and fearful. Yet, ironically, that is exactly what the Great Commission has called every believer to do. It tells us to go (Matt. 28:19) to the spiritually lost; it doesn't tell the spiritually lost to come to us.

So we need to be ready to share the gospel boldly, kindly, and confidently with people when opportunities arise. But what about the fear factor of being a soul winner? Two things are needed to replace fear with confidence. Number one and most important, you need the holy boldness that only comes from the Holy Spirit. Second, you need regular coaching and practice to share the gospel. Just like in sports, good coaching and good practice lead to great execution.

Many leaders can tend to become dull soul winners if they're not actively sharpening their zeal and ability to articulate the gospel. How are you being led and coached in the gospel? It will be difficult to lead and coach others if you're not having people lead and coach you in the gospel. Also, how are you leading and coaching yourself? Read books on apologetics, listen to podcasts on cultural questions, and familiarize yourself with personal evangelism tools and strategies.

Then, there is also a call to disciple and coach others in the gospel. As one called to ministry, you are charged with an all-important task to "equip the saints for the work of ministry, to build up the body of Christ" (Eph. 4:12). You can't assume the people in your ministry know how to share the gospel just because they've been coming to church. Many people know how to share pieces of the gospel but struggle to share the entire gospel. As leaders, it's our job to coach and train them to share the whole gospel—creation, sin, Jesus's life, crucifixion, burial, resurrection, ascension, return and redemption of all things, plus the call on people to repent and believe. So pick an evangelism tool and coach people to use it.

One of the most common questions Scott and I get is, What is the best evangelism tool to train people? It's a great question. An important one. Here is how we always reply: "The best evangelism tool is the one that shares the gospel and that the people will actually use." No one will know your context better than you do, so find the right evangelism tool for your context. Learn it

> A fearless Christian with the gospel is a soul winner.

yourself and coach others in it. Then practice saying it repeatedly. Say it aloud so that you can hear it yourself. Practice with other believers—share the gospel with them, then have them share with you. Practicing with other Christians is a safe space. If someone says something wrong or stumbles all over themselves, it's okay because you've provided a safe place to practice and coach others in getting more confident and clearer in what they're saying. Repetition in sharing the gospel builds confidence, and confidence helps dispel fear. A fearless Christian with the gospel is a soul winner.

Co-Mission Is the Calling

The Great Commission is one of the most beautiful callings in the Bible. It's not the Great Suggestion or even the Great Obligation. It's the Great Commission that is really a Great Invitation. The prefix *co-* means "with, together, joint heir." Think about that for a second. The Lord doesn't need anything or anyone—it's his creation, his message, and his mission. Yet he is inviting us to do it together with him. He doesn't need us to accomplish his mission, but he also doesn't want to do it without us. He is inviting us to come along on a journey with him while accomplishing his mission together. How incredible is that! As leaders, we get to be a part of his plan and get to equip others to be a part of it as well. All believers are called to be in this co-mission.

All believers have the Holy Spirit inside them. Each believer is a minister of the gospel and a missionary. This includes both you and the people you're called to minister to. All Christians are called to live on mission! In 2 Corinthians, Paul told the whole church (not just the pastors) that "everything is from God, who has reconciled us to himself through Christ and has given us the *ministry* of reconciliation" (2 Cor. 5:18). Every church member has a ministry and a mission field. The church isn't a building to be maintained; it's a people to be mobilized.

How can we discover our daily ministry and mission fields? Simple. It's the ground beneath your feet at any point in the day. As a minister, you get to help others see that their school is more than a place to learn, their job is more than a place to work, and their family is more than just people who annoy them. The mission field is everywhere.

People are looking for eternal hope even if they don't realize it. Every single day there is a broken world outside the walls of our church buildings. That world left to its own devices is hopeless, joyless, ravaged by death, and full of conflict. A hopeless world needs hope, a joyless world needs joy, a world ravaged by death needs life, and a world full of conflict needs peace. As Christians, we know that hope has a name, joy has a name, life has a name, and peace has a name. That name is Jesus! "There is salvation in no one else, for there is no other name under heaven given to people by which we must be saved" (Acts 4:12).

What a great invitation, indeed! We get to go on a co-mission with Christ to tell the world that you're not too lost for Jesus to find, too dirty for Jesus to cleanse, too broken for Jesus to fix, too wounded for Jesus to heal, too far gone for Jesus to reach, too guilty for Jesus to forgive, or too sinful for Jesus to save!

You get to be a soul winner and disciple other believers in that same invitation. As Greg Stier points out, "Leaders worth following are ordinary people, courageously living out gospel advancing values."[4]

Soul winners are entrusted with something Amazon can't deliver—the lifesaving, world-changing, and soul-transforming message of Jesus Christ. You have the cure for the most dangerous disease there is—sin. That cure is the gospel. After all, can we really say that Jesus is the most important Person in our life if we refuse to talk about him?

CHAPTER 6

Loving the Church

People have a broad range of opinions about the most trivial things in life. Sometimes they can even be defensive and adamant about their views on topics that are ultimately meaningless. Admittedly, I (Scott) have found myself in more than one debate about which toppings are appropriate for pizza, whether a dog or cat makes the best pet, or debates about which athlete is the GOAT (greatest of all time) in their respective sport.

In the same way, the much more significant concept of "church" typically evokes a variety of passionate responses. Some people are nostalgic and sentimental in the way they view church. Others may have a ceremonial perspective that derives from a religious and formal understanding. For some, the mention of "church" opens wounds of disappointment or hurt that they associate with previous experiences. Sadly, some of the strongest (and the most common!)

opinions about the church are more accusatory and associate church with an institutional religion that is corrupt or a house of hypocrites who are judgmental and self-righteous.

While the church and her members are certainly not perfect, we cannot base our view of the church on personal opinions, past experiences, unrealistic expectations, or a naïve understanding. As you consider your calling, it is essential to understand how it relates to and ultimately serves God's church. The Bible defines the church with three primary metaphors that describe the spiritual reality of its nature, how it functions, and our particular role within it.[1]

The Body of Christ: *Gifted and Growing*

Perhaps the most common depiction of the church in the New Testament is its identification as the body of Christ. The apostle Paul repeatedly uses this phrase in his letters, most likely because of his conversion encounter with the resurrected Lord on the road to Damascus (Acts 9:1–6). In his confrontation, Jesus equates the "threats and murder" of his disciples (9:1) with personal persecution against him: "I am Jesus, the one you are persecuting" (9:5). As a result, Paul understands that believers constitute the spiritual body of Christ, and he provides practical instruction according to this reality in many of his letters.

The descriptive identity of the church as "the body" emphasizes the spiritual unity of believers as the living, growing, and function-ing people of Christ. In both the global and local sense, we are "one body" that consists of many members, each operating accord-ing to our specific role, collectively working together in unity and harmony to accomplish Christ's mission (1 Cor. 12:12–27; Rom. 12:4–5). This understanding of the church as the body of Christ provides the basis for some crucial theological and practical truths related to our calling.

Spiritual Gifts

As those called to ministry leadership, we must identify and serve the body of Christ according to our spiritual gifts. Many of the passages related to "the body" center around this important, but often neglected, subject. The topic of spiritual gifts is avoided in many churches because of confusion about what they are, debate about how they function, and concern over their possible misuse. But for the body of Christ to function properly, we must have a basic and biblical understanding of spiritual gifts that enables us to serve according to our giftedness.

A spiritual gift is a tangible expression of God's grace in the life of every believer that each one of us has a spiritual responsibility to use (1 Pet. 4:10; 1 Cor. 12:7). We must be careful not to confuse spiritual gifts with natural talents. The primary differences are that spiritual gifts are received at conversion, they cannot be manufactured or acquired, and God's Spirit enables and empowers us to use them (1 Cor. 12:11). Since God graciously and strategically distributes them, we should not envy others for their gifts or elevate those with more prominent gifts. Instead, we should value everyone's giftedness and be grateful for the spiritual gift(s) we receive, while together pursuing the "greater gifts" (1 Cor. 12:31) of "faith, hope, and love" (1 Cor. 13:13).

Scripture provides multiple lists that are representative of spiritual gifts and indicate how they function within the body of Christ (1 Cor. 12:8–10; Rom. 12:6–8). Although they are not formally classified as such, it's helpful to categorize spiritual gifts according to their purpose. For instance, speaking gifts (prophecy and teaching) involve proclaiming the truth of Scripture "as one who speaks God's words," while serving gifts (ministry and leadership) describe those who serve "from the strength God provides" (1 Pet. 4:11). Sign gifts (healing and miracles) are those that are intended to be evidence of God's power for missional purposes (1 Cor. 14:22), to proclaim the gospel (Acts 2:1–13; 8:12–13), and as a divine testimony of its life-changing power (Heb. 2:4). Scripture teaches that all spiritual gifts must function according to their intended purpose "decently and in order" (1 Cor. 14:40), for "the common good" of the body of Christ (1 Cor. 12:7), and with the ultimate goal of glorifying Jesus "in everything" (1 Pet. 4:11).

As we pursue our calling, it is important for us to explore our gifts to determine how the Lord desires to use us. There are some helpful resources such as spiritual gifts inventories that are available online or through your local church. But the best ways to identify your gifts is to survey the biblical lists while you begin to serve according to your interests, abilities, desires, and opportunities. This will provide internal confirmation while also giving others the chance to observe and affirm your giftedness. The Lord will confirm your gifts and calling through a deep sense of fulfillment, a desire for continued growth, and spiritual fruit for your labor.

In addition to exploring our gifts, we must also exercise our gifts. While spiritual gifts can't be manufactured, they can be developed and strengthened. Some gifts, like the gift of teaching, require a level of spiritual maturity and understanding that come with time and diligent study. Other gifts may not be initially discerned. They may become apparent when ministry opportunities arise and we make ourselves available to God. We may even identify our gifts and not have an immediate opportunity to use them. But as we discern our spiritual gifts, we have the responsibility to develop them in order to be prepared and proficient in our service to the Lord.

Finally, as we explore and exercise our gifts, we must employ our spiritual gifts in the body of Christ.[2] No matter what age or stage of life we're in, we must actively use our gifts to serve. This is especially important as you're discerning your call. This may mean that you need to ask for direction or permission from current ministry leaders as you look for opportunities or places to serve. It may mean that you should consider transitioning out of a current place of service that is helpful but doesn't allow you to use your gifts. And as you look for the right opportunity, be mindful that there are a variety of ministries and activities for your gifts and your service doesn't have to fit into a certain type of role (1 Cor. 14:4–6).

For those who are called to ministry leadership, discerning our spiritual gifts equips us to help others discern and serve according to theirs. In ministry, we live in a constant state of recruiting and deploying our members for service. Sometimes, as immediate needs arise, we can be tempted to simply "plug a hole" and fill a spot with someone who is willing. But the body of Christ will only function properly when every member is valued and when each one is fulfilling their intended purpose (1 Cor. 12:12–24). Helping people serve in areas that use their spiritual gifts is healthier for them, for the individual ministries, and for the body as a whole.

Spiritual Growth

In addition to spiritual gifts, our calling as ministry leaders within the body of Christ requires us to pursue and promote spiritual growth. Just as our physical bodies grow, the church as Christ's body should mature and develop. In Ephesians 4:12–16, God's Word repeatedly uses terms and phrases that emphasize the nature of this growth, its desired goal, and our role in the process.

The passage begins by identifying leadership roles that are designed for the specific purpose of equipping God's people for the work of ministry, "to *build up* the body of Christ" (Eph. 4:12, emphasis added). Our ultimate role is to promote the spiritual growth of individual members that results in a unified, corporate "maturity" and full "stature" (Eph. 4:13–14). As the body of Christ is established in the truth, we are called to "*grow* in every way" into Christ, who is "the head of the body" (Eph. 4:15; Col. 1:18, emphasis added). As the supreme authority, Jesus is the one who ultimately governs and guides his church. And, as

> Sometimes, as immediate needs arise, we can be tempted to simply "plug a hole" and fill a spot with someone who is willing. But the body of Christ will only function properly when every member is valued and when each one is fulfilling their intended purpose.

members of his body, we are all united together, different parts who collectively function to promote the "*growth* of the body for *building itself up*," each of us benefiting from what every member contributes (Eph. 4:16, emphasis added).

The growth of the body of Christ repeatedly emphasized throughout this passage is multifaceted. In one sense, this growth describes the breadth and width of the church as it expands through the global spread of the gospel and making disciples (Col. 1:6). This happens when the arms and hands of the body are reaching out and serving those in need and when the feet of the body are carrying the good news of Jesus everywhere we go. In another sense, the growth describes the depth of the church as it deepens its spiritual knowledge and understanding, with our hearts and minds becoming securely anchored in truth. The growth also includes the height of the church as we mature, becoming more like Jesus and functioning to serve and honor him!

The growth of the body of Christ is not only multifaceted; it is also multidimensional. Scripture speaks both on the spiritual growth of each individual member and on the collective growth of the body as a whole. The two certainly are related and operate in a way that is mutually beneficial and dependent on each other. The growth of the body will be facilitated by the growth of its individual members. The progress of the whole will also provide the nourishment and encouragement that help fuel the personal growth of each member. This growth translates into the local and global dimensions of the body. As growth occurs on the local level, the global church expands. As the global body of Christ grows, churches are planted and strengthened.

The body of Christ is beautiful. Its unity, diversity, and functionality, all operating in harmony, make it a unique family that is joined together by our common faith in Jesus. Our calling to vocational ministry provides the unique privilege of serving, supporting, and strengthening the body of Christ.

The Bride of Christ: *Loving and Leading*

In addition to being the body of Christ, the Bible identifies the church as the bride of Christ. Scripture reveals that earthly marriage is ultimately a reflection of a heavenly reality, the covenant relationship between Jesus, the Bridegroom, and his bride, the church (Gen. 2:24–25; Eph. 5:31–32; Rev. 19:6–9). As the bride of Christ, the church's relationship with him is characterized by two primary characteristics—redemptive love and trustworthy leadership. These attributes should inform our understanding and shape our approach to ministry as we pursue our calling to serve the bride of Christ.

Before we consider the practical implications of our calling, we must recognize that we are first and foremost part of his bride. As those called to vocational ministry, we do not occupy some unique status or position between Christ and his people. We are not his "best man" or the church's "maid of honor." We are members of his bride. Our first priority is to relish our personal relationship with Jesus as the loving Bridegroom who has redeemed and rescued us. As fellow members of his bride, we need Christ's renewal to purify and refine our hearts, meaning we must adopt the mindset that the sanctifying work of Christ's bride includes (and begins with!) us.

At the same time, we also have the privilege of loving and leading God's people in a way that reflects the heart of Jesus for his bride. Ephesians 5:22–33 establishes parallels for a husband's relationship with his wife that reflect Christ's relationship with his bride. This text also provides practical insights for us as we seek to emulate Jesus's love and leadership in our ministry to his bride.

Loving His Bride

Christ's love for his church provides the model for our faithfulness and devotion to her. As husbands are commanded to love their wives, the guiding standard is "as Christ loved the church," and the extent of his love is epitomized by the ultimate sacrifice, "and gave himself for her" (Eph. 5:25). The ultimate worth of the church as Christ's bride should provoke a deeper love within our hearts for God's people. While they are not always lovable, they are precious to our Savior, and we should treat them accordingly. Ministry is messy, people can be petty, and our work can seem worthless. But in the moments when these realities begin to dominate our perspective, we must renew our devotion to his bride because she is so dear to him.

While our lives are not the atoning sacrifice for them, we are called to love them to the same sacrificial extent. Jesus commanded us, "Love one another as I have loved you," and he characterized this love with its ultimate expression: "No one has greater love than this: to lay down his life for his friends" (John 15:12–13). In the same way that Jesus "lays down his life for the sheep" (John 10:11), our calling requires us to sacrifice our lives for his people. This may mean that we adjust our lifestyle for the financial health of the church or that we adjust our schedule to accommodate the ministry needs of the church. At the very least, it will certainly involve us laying aside our personal pride as we endure unrealistic expectations, unfair assumptions, and unkind encounters within the church. And, in the most difficult circumstances, it could mean that we should step down from our position for the sake of preserving and protecting Christ's bride.

The sacrificial love of Christ for his bride also serves a sanctifying purpose. Through his atoning and redemptive work on the cross, he cleanses his bride to "make her holy" and to present her to himself "in splendor, without spot or wrinkle" in order that she might become "holy and blameless" (Eph. 5:26–27). As we love the church, our desire should be to see God's people, individually and collectively, transformed into the likeness of Jesus. We should love people as they are, with all their burdens and baggage, but we should love them enough to help them become all that Christ calls them to be. This means that we must always keep in mind—the sanctifying process of the church has not been completed. In ministry, you will face plenty of wrinkles and blemishes within the church, but we are serving Christ and his bride to help iron them out and clear them up.

Both our motives and our methods should reflect the love of Christ. Jesus's relationship with the church is characterized by tenderness and mercy as he lovingly nourishes and cares for his bride, selflessly and sacrificially providing for her needs (Eph. 5:29). Likewise, we must extend grace, show mercy, and be patient with people and allow the Lord to work in their lives. Loving the bride of Christ with sacrificial and sanctifying love that reflects his is hard.

Unspeakably hard. But the immeasurable worth of his bride makes our service to her worth every effort!

Leading His Bride

Along with his redemptive love, the church as the bride of Christ reflects his trustworthy leadership. While Christ's love for the church is the motivation for his sacrifice and sanctifying care, the Ephesians passage begins by describing the leadership that Jesus provides for his bride. The instruction to wives reflects our willing submission to Christ as the "head of the church" (Eph. 5:22–24). But his positional authority as the "head" does not simply demand compliance. As the "Savior of the body" (v. 23), he has demonstrated that he is completely trustworthy. Therefore, we can confidently follow his leadership in loving obedience.

While Christ has ultimate authority over his people, we are called to exercise trustworthy leadership that compels them to a deeper obedience to Christ (Heb. 13:17; 1 Pet. 5:3). This type of leadership begins with character and integrity. These traits are essential in life, but they are crucial for ministry. As leaders, our lives should reflect the character of Christ as those who are being transformed by his grace into his image (2 Cor. 3:18). In doing so, we provide a godly example for others to follow (1 Cor. 11:1). But beyond our imperfect attempts to model Christ for our people, character and integrity provide the basis for their trust.

In addition to being trustworthy, Christ's leadership is characterized by the ministry of the Word that cleanses and sanctifies his bride (Eph. 5:26–27). Scripture must, then, be a distinguishing feature of our leadership. As we devote ourselves to preaching and

teaching his Word, God will wash and renew his people, individually and collectively, so that he may present his bride to himself in
radiant splendor. In ministry, we can try to motivate and manufacture change in people, but God's Word is the means by which he
sanctifies them.

As those who are called to ministry, we must commit ourselves
to honoring the bride of Christ with leadership that is trustworthy
and biblically sound. These characteristics are developed over time
and require our own continued progress in personal holiness and
devotion to his Word. But these commitments won't last unless
they flow from our sincere affection for his bride. Ultimately,
like Christ's covenant with his bride, love and leadership are wed
together. And they must also be in our lives and ministries.

The Building of Christ: *Presence and Purpose*

People often say, "The church is not a building; the church is
God's people!" Rightly motivated, this expression is meant to emphasize the personal and communal nature of the church. And while the
church is not simply a brick-and-mortar structure, Scripture teaches
us that, in addition to being the body and bride of Christ, we are
also the building of Christ. When the apostle Peter pronounced that
Jesus is "the Messiah, the Son of the living God," Jesus responded
with divine affirmation and a promise, "On this rock I will *build* my
church" (Matt. 16:16–18, emphasis added). In this assertion, Jesus
not only expressed his intention to establish a covenant community;
he confirmed the truth of his identity as its eternal foundation.

It shouldn't surprise us that, in his first letter, Peter identified Jesus as "the cornerstone" and his people as "living stones" being assembled and "built" into his "spiritual house" (1 Pet. 2:4–8). Likewise, Paul explicitly identifies us as "God's building" that is being constructed, and the "foundation is Jesus Christ" (1 Cor. 3:9–11). Elsewhere, we are called "members of God's household," being "built" on "Christ Jesus himself as the cornerstone" into "a holy temple in the Lord" (Eph. 2:19–21). As the building of Christ, our stability is through our mutual dependence on one another and the unshakable foundation of Christ himself. But, like the bride and the body, the building is not simply a metaphor. It is a spiritual reality that communicates other important truths that have practical implications for us as we pursue and fulfill our calling.

God's Presence and His People

Throughout Scripture, the distinguishing mark of God's people was his presence among them (Exod. 33:14–16). In the Old Testament, his presence was signified by the ark of the covenant, the tabernacle, and the temple. But in the New Testament, as believers in Christ, we are his temple as the Holy Spirit takes up residence within our individual hearts (1 Cor. 3:16–17; 6:19). Collectively, as his church, the Bible teaches us that we are "being built together for God's dwelling in the Spirit" (Eph. 2:22). This means that as the building of Christ, God's presence dwells within *and* among us!

Through Christ, God fulfilled his covenant promise to establish his people as his dwelling place. Indeed, "we are the temple of the living God," in which God promised, "I will dwell and walk among them, and I will be their God, and they will be my people. . . . I will welcome you. And I will be a Father to you, and you will be sons and daughters to me, says the Lord Almighty" (2 Cor. 6:16–18).

While it is not a physical structure made by hands (Acts 17:24), as the church, we are his building. This means that we exist as a spiritual community where our great God and King resides! Therefore, our personal interaction should be characterized by his kindness. Our ministries should display his selfless love and service. Our giving should his reflect immeasurable grace. And our worship should celebrate and bask in his glory!

God's Purpose for His People

God's presence is not without purpose. His presence has always been intended to be a testimony to the nations of his glory and grace. God's initial promise to Abraham was that his covenant people would become a blessing to the nations (Gen. 12:1–3). When Solomon dedicated the temple, his prayer expressed God's intention to use it as a testimony of his presence to the nations (1 Kings 8:60). In the same way, God declared to the prophet Isaiah that his house should be called "a house of prayer for all nations" (Isa. 56:7).

The redemptive work of Christ is intended to serve a missional purpose. We are called to "make disciples of all nations" as we carry out the Great Commission, and he has assured us, "I am with you always" (Matt. 28:18–20). As God's people, we are "a chosen race, a royal priesthood, a holy nation, a people for his possession" for the expressed purpose of proclaiming the excellencies of "the one who called [us] out of darkness into his marvelous light" (1 Pet. 2:9). The gospel message is a global message that will culminate in "a vast multitude from every nation, tribe, people, and language" worshipping Christ around his throne (Rev. 7:9–10). This means that God has established us as his people for this purpose.

Practically speaking, we have the responsibility to cultivate a spiritual community that relishes our identity as Christ's building. As those who are called to ministry, we have the divine privilege of serving in God's house. Therefore, we should celebrate his presence in and among us, proclaim the gospel to the lost, and invite them to join with us, to be a part of Christ's church.

Conclusion

Each of the biblical pictures of the church provides specific insights for us as we pursue our calling. The strength and unity of the body of Christ should challenge us to serve with our gifts, value every member as we enlist them to do the same, and promote the spiritual growth of God's people into the fullness and likeness of Jesus. The radiance and splendor of the bride of Christ should stimulate our affections for the church and inspire us to care for her with sacrificial love and trustworthy leadership. And as we welcome God's presence within and among us as the building of Christ, we must devote ourselves to fulfilling his missional purpose for the church.

Our commitment to the church will be tested. Maintaining a biblical perspective of God's people can guard our hearts from becoming jaded or cynical toward them in those challenging seasons. As those who are called to a lifetime of service to the church, we must continue to foster a deep and abiding love for the body, the bride, and the building of Christ!

CHAPTER 7

Relying on the Spirit

Growing up on the coast of North Carolina, I (Scott) was exposed to a "surf and sand" lifestyle that included a lot of unique elements. But there are some aspects of the beach life that don't require a coastal upbringing for people to grasp. For instance, sailboats are one of those universal objects that everyone can easily identify and understand. The term itself perfectly describes their identity and function. They range from a relatively small watercraft to massive ships. While their size and purpose may differ, they all operate on the same basic principle. The concept of using wind to propel a vessel across the water is easily understood. And since everyone knows what the wind feels like, sailing can be easily imagined. But the truth is, most people have never personally experienced the exhilaration of sailing.

Similarly, when it comes to the person and work of the Holy Spirit, many Christians are aware of his presence and have "felt the wind," but most believers don't know how to "sail." Tragically, many in the church are just floating along in the harbor of life with their spiritual sails down or trying to propel themselves forward by blowing into them. These futile attempts to sail mirror the absurdity of trying to live the Christian life apart from the power of the Spirit; it's impossible!

In addition to our own spiritual walk, to successfully chart a course through the shifting tides and open waters of ministry, we must be propelled by the Spirit. But this requires us to understand who he is, what he does, and how we can position our sails to be controlled and led by him. This begins by understanding and affirming some foundational truths about his nature and his work.[1]

Scripture teaches that there is one true and living God who exists in three persons—the Father, the Son, and the Holy Spirit. The Spirit is fully God, identical in essence and eternal in nature (Heb. 9:14). He is equated with the Father and the Son (Matt. 28:19; 2 Cor. 13:14) and actively participates in the divine work of salvation (Eph. 1:3–14). While commonly misunderstood as some impersonal force or mysterious power, the Spirit is a distinct person of the triune God.[2]

As believers, we are converted by the work of the Spirit (John 3:1–7; 1 Tim. 3:5), our salvation is permanently sealed by the Spirit (Eph 1:13-14), and the Spirit of God dwells in us (1 Cor. 6:19–20). We are sanctified by the Spirit (1 Pet. 1:2), gifted by the Spirit (1 Cor. 12:11), and empowered by the Spirit (Eph. 3:16). In other words, there's nothing God does in our lives that is not accomplished by his Spirit!

Yet, despite his divine nature and comprehensive role, the person and work of the Spirit are often neglected because many people lack a biblical understanding of his nature and role. It is a sad reality for many believers, but it is a tragedy for those called to ministry. For us, ignoring the Spirit will not only cripple our walk; it will disable our work. As Spurgeon rightly asserts, "To us, as ministers, the Holy Spirit is absolutely essential."[3] Apart from the Spirit, our work for the Lord will be an empty attempt to manufacture spiritual results through our own futile efforts. Therefore, as we pursue our calling, we must learn what it means to walk in the Spirit and depend on him. Four foundational aspects of the Spirit's ministry to us serve as the essential building blocks of our ministry through him.

The Spirit Is Our Companion

Hours before his crucifixion, Jesus told his disciples that his death and departure were imminent. But as he prepared to leave them, he assured them that he would not leave them alone. Jesus promised that God would send "another Helper" like him "to be *with you forever*" (John 14:16 ESV, emphasis added). The comfort of the Spirit's eternal companionship was reinforced through the assurance of the personal and abiding nature of his presence: "He remains *with you* and will be *in you*" (John 14:17, emphasis added). Because of the Spirit's indwelling nature and his divine power and universal presence, Jesus explained to his disciples that it was beneficial for him to depart and send the Spirit (John 16:7).

When Jesus ascended into heaven, he fulfilled his promise and sent the Holy Spirit to reside in and among his people. So now, when we trust in Christ, we are not only assured that we will dwell with him eternally, but he also assures us that he will dwell in us personally. As a result, the Spirit is our companion in life and for ministry. And his abiding presence reassures us with some important truths that bolster our faith and strengthen our confidence.

First, as we pursue our calling, we can be certain that *the Spirit walks with us*. Throughout our life and ministry, we have God's promise that we are not alone. The Spirit is our trustworthy traveling companion who reassures us of his divine presence. Just as God encouraged Joshua in his preparation to inherit the promised land, we can be strong and courageous because we have the Spirit as our divine guide who walks behind us, beside us, and before us (Deut. 31:8).

His presence is essential because ministry can be terrifying and lonely. Few recognize the weight and emotional strains ministers carry. We can often feel isolated or misunderstood. Loneliness arises because we can struggle to have in-depth relationships, especially with those we serve, as we try to balance leadership and appropriate levels of transparency. In difficult seasons, it's particularly challenging because we can feel abandoned or targeted by people's frustration. But the Spirit's presence is with us. He will strengthen us, and he will help us (Isa. 41:10).

In addition to walking with us, we are assured that *the Spirit watches over us*. Along with his divine presence, we can rely on the

Spirit for his provision and protection. His provision is necessary because when we surrender to God's call to ministry, we trust him to provide for our physical, emotional, and spiritual needs. The apostle Paul learned how to be content and to rely on the Lord to meet every need, and he assures us, "My God will supply all your needs according to his riches in glory in Christ Jesus" (Phil. 4:19). He also reminds us that through the Spirit his grace is sufficient for all our needs as well (Eph. 3:16; 2 Cor. 12:9–10).

The Spirit also offers us protection from our spiritual and worldly enemies. We are stewards of the gospel and our gifts, and through the Holy Spirit we are challenged to guard the treasure that has been entrusted to us (2 Tim. 1:14). But the security we have in our ministries is not the result of our strength or wisdom; it's only because, like Paul, we can say, "I know whom I have believed and am persuaded that *he* is able to guard what has been entrusted to me until that day" (2 Tim. 1:12, emphasis added). The spiritual battles against the flesh, the culture, and the adversary all require the power of God's Spirit to protect us.

As he walks with us and watches over us, the Bible also promises that *the Spirit works through us.* At some level we all struggle with insecurities and inadequacies, especially when we recognize the magnitude of our calling. While we know that the redemptive work of Christ affirms our personal value and qualifies us to be used by God, our inabilities can cause us to question our practical value. But as we saw in the previous chapter on the church, the Spirit equips us with spiritual gifts to fulfill God's will for our lives. Through us the Spirit accomplishes God's work beyond what we could ever achieve in our own strength or ability.

Paul's familiar prayer for the Ephesians highlights this point even though it is often overlooked when we reference it: "Now to him who is able to do above and beyond all that we ask or think according to the power that works *in us*" (Eph. 3:20, emphasis added). Earlier in his prayer Paul identified the source of his power and strength within us as "his Spirit" (Eph. 3:16), and now he emphasizes the unbelievable reality that the supernatural work that exceeds our imagination will be accomplished by his Spirit working through *us*. What an amazing privilege! But the gratitude and joy that flood our hearts ultimately doesn't celebrate us. It overflows in continuous praise to the One who graciously works in and through us (Eph. 3:21).

Perhaps the greatest work God performs through us is allowing us to participate in his redeeming work as we share the gospel. And the Spirit's role is instrumental in our evangelism efforts. In fact, prior to his ascension, Jesus promised that the Spirit would empower us to be his witnesses as we proclaim the gospel message and fulfill his global mission (Acts 1:8). The Spirit not only gives us boldness and courage to share the good news, but he's also the only one who can remove the veil and penetrate the darkness of the human heart with the light of the gospel that leads people to faith in Christ (2 Cor. 3:16–17; 4:2–6). Our confidence to share the good news is not based on our persuasive ability; it's founded entirely on the power of the gospel and the promise of the Spirit to work through us!

Since the Spirit is our companion, we can live and serve with confidence knowing that he walks with us, watches over us, and works through us. As we navigate the challenges of life, but particularly those in ministry, each of these truths will be essential as we learn to lean on him.

The Spirit Is Our Counselor

When Jesus promised that he would send the Spirit, he identified him as the "Counselor" (John 14:16). Jesus repeatedly refers to him with this title to describe his multifaceted ministry (John 14:26; 15:26; 16:7). The term *Paraclete*, which literally means "the one called alongside,"[4] conveys multiple aspects of his divine assistance. In addition to "Counselor" (csb), different translations use a variety of terms to capture the essential elements of his nature, including "Helper" (esv), "Comforter" (kjv), and "advocate" (niv). Collectively, these various translations provide us with a greater understanding of the breadth and depth of his ministry.

One of the more distinctive aspects of his role is captured by the commonly used term "Counselor." This translation emphasizes his divine guidance that counsels us as we follow God's will. Jesus clarifies this title with the explanation of the Spirit's role to "teach" (John 14:26) and "guide" us (John 16:13). The Spirit is our reliable and trustworthy leader who helps us discern God's plan for our lives and navigate the journey along the way. As we pursue our calling, there are two primary aspects of his guidance that we can trust.

First, as our Counselor, *the Spirit guides us with direction*. Throughout the New Testament, we see the compelling role of the Spirit in guiding our lives. When Jesus initially explained salvation to Nicodemus, he declared that we must be "born of the Spirit," and when we are, like how the wind blows, we will be directed by

the Spirit (John 3:1–8). Likewise, throughout the book of Acts, we
see the Spirit directing God's servants as they pursued their calling
(Acts 8:29; 11:12; 13:4; 16:6–10; 20:22). In the same way, we are
called to be "led by the Spirit" (Gal. 5:18).

The Spirit's guidance provides direction as we face various decisions throughout our life and ministry. It includes personal choices
as we consider options related to our vocational calling and the
trajectory of our lives. It also involves practical and daily choices as
we determine what God is leading us to do. The Spirit's guidance
also directs our pursuits in ministry as we identify next steps in
following God's will. This may include leadership decisions for our
ministries or personal decisions as we transition from one ministry
platform to a new one.

But being "led by the Spirit" can't just be ministry lingo used
to justify our decisions. Following the Spirit's guidance requires us
to avoid confusing our desires with his direction. This clarification
comes through prayerful reflection, seeking wisdom from other
faithful believers, and filtering our options through Scripture. It
also comes through faith as we trust him with wholehearted obedience, and allow him to "direct [our] paths" (Prov. 3:5–6 KJV).

In addition to direction, *the Spirit guides us with discernment*.
So much of life and ministry come down to exercising sound judgment and practical wisdom. Obviously, more leaders and ministries
have failed from of a lack of godly wisdom and discernment than
they have from moral collapse. Sadly, a primary factor is their failure to recognize our need for the Spirit's guidance for wisdom and
discernment.

Practically speaking, using discernment means that we live according to God's standards rather than the world's perspective. Speaking biblically, this is described as living according to wisdom "from above" instead of wisdom from below (James 3:13–18). But this type of discernment and understanding is only possible through the Spirit. Scripture is clear: God reveals spiritual things to us "by the Spirit," and apart from the Spirit it is impossible for us to comprehend God's will and his ways (1 Cor. 2:10–16). So, to live according to God's wisdom, we must listen to the "Spirit of wisdom" (Eph. 1:17).

Jesus's promise to send the Counselor included further clarification of his role as the One who would guide us with discernment. Specifically, he promised that the Spirit will "guide [us] into all the truth" as he speaks and declares God's will to us (John 16:13–15). The Spirit also teaches us all things (John 14:26) as he leads us according to the Scriptures he inspired (2 Pet. 1:20–21). In other words, the Spirit's discernment and wisdom are accessed, dispensed, and confirmed through the timeless truth of God's Word. Therefore, we lean on the Spirit's discernment by evaluating our lives and the world around us through the lens of Scripture.

From our life's perspective, the Spirit's discernment is necessary to help navigate moral decisions, ethical issues, cultural politics, relational dynamics, and situational dilemmas. In leadership, his discernment provides wisdom as we minister to people in difficult circumstances, discern people's spiritual condition and corresponding needs, manage and mobilize people for service, assess complex and unforeseen situations, and determine how to propel our ministries forward. Thankfully, God graciously provides us the direction and discernment we need through the work and wisdom of his Spirit!

The Spirit Is Our Comforter

Like his work as our Counselor, the Spirit also serves as our Comforter. Along with his divine guidance, Jesus identified the Spirit with elements of ministry and encouragement. This is astounding for us to understand because as we minster to others in the name of Christ, the Spirit ministers to us on Christ's behalf! There are multiple aspects of his ministry as our Comforter that are especially significant because of the unique challenges that come with our calling.

For example, ministry leadership often requires us to carry the spiritual and emotional weight of the people we serve (2 Cor. 11:28). As a result of our empathy and responsibility, our hearts can become troubled, unsettled, and even overwhelmed. The burdens that we help shoulder for others (Gal. 6:2) are compounded by our own personal struggles that we must carry for ourselves (Gal. 6:5). This can drain us physically, emotionally, and spiritually. It not only can cause us to feel spiritually dry and weary, but ultimately it can result in ministry burnout. But in those moments or seasons of distress, *the Spirit is our source of peace.*

Immediately following Jesus's promise to send the Spirit (John 14:26), he commends his supernatural peace to his disciples, "My peace I give to you," and he reassures them, "Don't let your heart be troubled or fearful" (John 14:27). God's Spirit in our hearts provides us with his peace in multiple ways. He supplies us with peace as part of the spiritual fruit he produces in our lives (Gal. 5:22). He quiets our hearts and minds as we fix them on him (Rom. 8:5–6; cf. Isa. 26:3). And even when we are so overwhelmed that we don't know how to pray, the Spirit intervenes in our weakness and intercedes for us (Rom. 8:26–27). As the Spirit guides our prayers, our humble dependence on God can dispel our anxious thoughts and "the peace of God, which surpasses all understanding, will guard [our] hearts and our minds in Christ Jesus" (Phil. 4:6–7).

In addition to being our source of peace, *the Spirit is our strength to persevere.* Many people cling to the empty premise that "God won't give me more than I can handle." But that statement is incomplete. Many challenges in our lives and ministries will overwhelm us and require more physical and emotional strength than any of us possess. But, while there are endless situations we can't manage on our own, nothing is impossible with his help.

The ministry of the Spirit is vital because his supernatural power that dwells within us corresponds with the strength that our life and ministry require. Paul recognized our need for dependence on him and fittingly prayed for the Ephesians "to be *strengthened with power* in your inner being *through his Spirit*" (Eph. 3:16, emphasis added). He also understood the necessity of our reliance on his immense power to stand firm through the intensity of the spiritual battles we endure in life and ministry (Eph. 6:10–12). But in our weakness God's strength is perfected (2 Cor. 12:9) through the ministry of his Spirit, since "God has not given us a spirit of fear, but one of *power*, love, and sound judgment" (2 Tim. 1:7).

As our source of peace and strength, the Spirit's ministry as our Comforter provides us with everything we need for the heartaches and hardships in life and ministry. Peace isn't found in the absence of difficulty; it's found in the presence of God as we walk through them. By faith we can cling to the promise of Paul's prayer for the Romans, "Now may the God of hope fill you with all joy and *peace* as you believe so that you may overflow with hope by the *power* of the Holy Spirit" (Rom. 15:13).

The Spirit Is Our Conqueror

As our Conqueror, the Spirit enables us to experience victory as we battle the temptations of the flesh and seek to grow in our faith. Because of his divine power and presence, *by the Spirit we can defeat the sinful flesh.* Although we often feel weak when facing temptations, we are not left to face our struggles alone. The Spirit empowers us to overcome them through the work Christ has already accomplished on our behalf. Because he has rescued us from the power and penalty of sin (Rom. 6:1–11), we can present ourselves to God as "slaves to righteousness" (Rom. 6:12–19). Still, even though the gospel transforms our positional status before God, the presence of sin remains and continues to wage war within our hearts (Rom. 7:14–25). In essence, we are prisoners of war, held captive in this "body of death" (Rom. 7:24).

But through the Spirit we have the power of Christ's resurrection dwelling in us to give us new life in him (Rom. 8:1–11). Therefore, "we are not obligated to the flesh," and "by the Spirit" we can overcome the sinful cravings of the flesh (Rom. 8:12–14). This doesn't mean we should recklessly seek to be tempted. Instead, we are to "flee" from sinfulness and pursue righteousness (2 Tim. 2:22;

1 Tim. 6:11). But when we are unable to avoid the enemy's attempts to entice us, we must cling to our identity in Christ and yield to the Spirit's power within us. His weapons are available to withstand the enemy's attacks, the "sword of the Spirit—which is the word of God" and our prayers as we "pray at all times in the Spirit" (Eph. 6:17–18). Therefore, we can be certain, when we "walk by the Spirit" we will "not carry out the desire of the flesh" (Gal. 5:16).

Along with defeating our sinful flesh, *by the Spirit we can produce spiritual fruit.* The work of the Spirit goes beyond simply keeping us from sin. As the Spirit wages war against the flesh and we are "led by the Spirit" (Gal. 5:16–18), he changes us from the inside out. Those who submit to the flesh are characterized by the rotten fruit of sinfulness (Gal. 5:19–21), but those controlled by the Spirit are distinguished by the ripe fruit of righteousness (Gal. 5:22–24). The Spirit transforms us into the likeness of Christ and produces character traits in us, "the fruit of the Spirit," that reflect his nature and behavior.

Any godly behavior in our lives is not the result of our own strength or effort. It's God's Spirit working in us. Before his death and departure, Jesus repeatedly connected the work of the Spirit to our ability to obey his word (John 14:15–17, 23–26). God does this by conforming us to the image of Christ through the work of the Spirit (2 Cor. 3:18; 1 Pet. 1:2). As we submit to the work of the Spirit, we must not quench him by disregarding or disobeying his voice (1 Thess. 5:19) or "grieve" him by willfully indulging sin (Eph. 4:30). Instead, we should cooperate with his transforming work by learning to rely on him in submission and obedience.

The Spirit's sanctifying work in our lives will be crucial as we fulfill our calling. As God's servants, we must devote ourselves to growing in Christlikeness so that we can become a holy and useful instrument in the hand of our Master. This ultimately enables us to be a godly and gentle example for his people and a credible and effective witness to the lost (2 Tim. 2:20–26). While the magnitude of this responsibility can seem overwhelming, we can rejoice because God has graciously given us his Spirit, the Conqueror, to make it possible!

Conclusion

The person and work of the Spirit is crucial for our success in life and ministry. His role as our Companion reassures us of his presence that walks with us, watches over us, and works through us. As our Counselor, he guides us with the discernment and direction we need to follow God's will and fulfill his calling on our lives. Through his ministry as our Comforter, he is our source of peace and our strength to persevere as we navigate the unique challenges of ministry. And, as our Conqueror, he works within us to defeat our sinful flesh and produce spiritual fruit.

In addition to the various ways he ministers to us, the Spirit also enables us to be used by him in similar capacities as we serve God's people. In reflection of his role as our Companion, we can come alongside others to walk with them and shepherd them with loving care. As we minister to our people through dark and difficult days, a ministry of presence often provides the reassurance they need. Additionally, as ministry leaders, people will often look to us for discernment and direction as they seek the Lord. Through the Spirit's role as our Counselor, we can share his guidance with them and teach them how to follow his leadership in their lives.

As our Comforter, the Spirit is the divine agent of God's mercies in our afflictions so that we can comfort others in theirs (2 Cor. 1:3–8). Although we don't have supernatural peace or divine strength to offer, our support reflects the Spirit's ministry and becomes an avenue for the peace and power that only he can provide. Similarly, we don't have the ability to personally fight their spiritual battles or produce spiritual fruit, but we are able to reflect the Spirit's ministry as we exhort them to grow in these areas. Through the Spirit's work in our lives, our ministries can encourage and equip them as they learn to rely on the Spirit as their Conqueror.

While we must learn to rely on the Spirt and allow him to work in and through us, we must also remember that his ultimate role is to glorify Christ (John 16:14). When we begin to celebrate our own abilities or achievements, we will stifle the Spirit's work in our lives and ministries since his purpose is to testify about our Savior and Lord (John 15:26). Therefore, we should cooperate with the Spirit and join him in his mission by directing everything he accomplishes in our lives and ministries to the praise and honor of Jesus. And when Christ is lifted up, the ultimate goal of our ministries will be accomplished as he draws all people to himself (John 12:32).

offer onstage. But if you're serving people well offstage, then it will only help them connect with you onstage.

Jesus's model of ministry was leading and influencing people by serving them. Serving people is the only way to minister to people. After all, the word minister literally means "servant." If you're not serving, you're not ministering.

Two great examples of servant leadership style are shown in John 13 and Philippians 2. In John 13, Jesus washes the disciples' feet. This would have been astonishing to a first-century Jewish person. It even caught Peter off guard so much that he didn't want Jesus to do it. As unappealing as washing someone's feet sounds today, imagine washing the feet of people who walked everywhere they went wearing sandals in a hot and dusty land filled with livestock and stepping in things that come out of livestock.

When people came into a house, it was customary for a servant to clean their feet so as to not make a mess inside. As you can imagine, it wasn't the most coveted job for servants. It was often the job of the servant at the bottom of the organizational chart to do this not-so-illustrious job. And yet here is the King of kings and Lord of lords taking on the job of the servant of all servants (John 13:4–5). Here is the bright and morning star (Rev. 22:16) taking the role of a servant. He set the example of service over stardom.

In the book of Philippians, Paul tells the church in Philippi to take on the attitude of serving others with humility and to place others above themselves by saying, "Do nothing out of selfish ambition or conceit, but in humility consider others as more important than yourselves. Everyone should look not to his own interests, but rather to the interests of others" (Phil. 2:3–4). Then, of course, the example he gives us to follow in this kind of attitude is none other than Jesus himself, when "instead he emptied himself by assuming the form of a servant" (Phil. 2:7). Jesus, who is God, served mankind in the most ultimate way possible by dying on a cross in our place (v. 8).

Jesus Christ is the most famous one of all, and yet he didn't have a rock-star attitude; he operated with a servant's attitude (Mark 10:45).

If he ministered to people as a servant, then that is the same model we must follow as leaders. Ultimately, the Son of God served us so that we would serve others (John 13:14–15). We're not called to ministry for stardom; we are called for service.

Real Servant Leaders and Sasquatch

Serving must come from the outflow of who you are as a servant. If you do not see yourself as a servant, then you'll attempt to serve people out of a sense of obligation, and it won't seem genuine. People tend to have a keen sense in spotting when leaders aren't being authentic servants. We don't like insincerity, and neither do they.

Through the calling of God and the power of the Holy Spirit, being a servant is who we authentically are, and serving is what we genuinely do out of a love for God and people. Dr. Iorg says, "Servant leadership is, in its essence, an attitude. Servant leadership is defined more by who you are than by what you do."[4]

In 2011, a documentary-drama series premiered on Animal Planet called *Finding Bigfoot*. A guy named Matt, who founded the Bigfoot Field Researchers Organization (BFRO), and his team of investigators traveled North America to search for the ever-elusive Sasquatch, more affectionately known as Bigfoot.

Early on it was easy to be enthralled by this show. It felt like you were a part of this "nerd herd," and you'd be on the hunt with them. While being on this journey with the experts from the BFRO crew, it felt like we were all going to finally find Bigfoot. Personally, my fascination lasted for a whole seven episodes, and then I realized that we were never going to find him.

Yet this team, along with millions of other people, continue to be convinced that he is real. Every broken branch, vague knocking sound, and flock of birds being scared by something was hard-core evidence for them that he was out there somewhere. I gave up, but they have continued for eleven whole seasons. Still no luck.

Just as most of us don't believe Bigfoot really exists, many people don't believe that *authentic* servants of the Lord really exist either. Is a good minister a myth? Are they urban legends that teams of hopeful people search for but eventually give up with no avail?

Here is the difference between a good Sasquatch and a good servant. Good servant leaders really do exist. They are out there and aren't that elusive. However, if one is found, the church should do its best to never let them go. The church must encourage the ones we have and help develop more of them. May this person be you, and may God use you to serve and raise up more genuine servants of Jesus and his bride.

Many churches and ministries have some great servant leaders. If you find a healthy church who has a good minister, you will know it. You can hear the evidence of that leader in their voices and see it in the lives of others. The effects of a good servant leader can be felt for generations to come.

Nevertheless, how do you know if you, yourself, have the characteristics of a servant of the Lord? How do you identify other servant leaders? What do these qualities and characteristics look like?

First, unlike what we may have been misled to believe by social media, conferences, denominations, and online ministry platforms, it has nothing to do with how large your church's membership is, how big your ministry budget is, or if you have a blue check next to your name with a hundred thousand followers on social media. It also has little to do with how gifted and talented the leader is, how articulate they are, or how trendy they dress.

There are some deeper distinctives and more important characteristics and qualities to look for. God has created and cultivated servant leaders to have the following.

Servant's Hands

A good servant leader has hands that are used for working hard (Ps. 90:17). Every minister has been gifted by God to serve the kingdom and to live sacrificially to place the bride of Christ above themselves. A good servant uses their hands for their God-called ministry, but they must also save some energy to use those hands to serve their family, their community, and other leaders they're calling out to also serve the kingdom.

Servant's Feet

A faithful servant has feet that follow Jesus. Any leader that is faithfully following Jesus is a leader worth following. The best spiritual leaders are those who are also the best spiritual followers (John 8:12).

Servant's Heart

A loving servant has a heart that beats with love for Jesus and for his church. The best way for a servant leader to faithfully love Christ's bride is for them to faithfully love the Groom, Jesus, with all their heart, soul, and mind (Matt. 22:37). Dr. Iorg writes, "Servant leadership is about the heart. It's primarily about motive. A servant leader is driven by his or her love for God and people."[5]

Servant's Mind

An effective servant has a pure mind that is not clouded by lustful thoughts for other people or other ministry positions. Their mind is not distracted with coveting their neighbor's possessions. In ministry, this can be the comparison trap. Be faithful to serve where the Lord has placed you, and do not get caught up in someone else's ministry assignment, social media following, or opportunities. Be thankful for and faithful with the assignment the sovereign God has given you. A servant has a mind that meditates on Scripture and is thankful for what the Lord has given him or her (2 Cor. 10:5).

Servant's Shoulders

A good servant leader has broad shoulders that aren't easily offended. He or she is strong enough to lovingly lead and be bold with the gospel, yet their shoulders are tender enough for people to cry on when they've been hurt, have experienced loss, or have come to a place of repentance over sin. Sometimes serving people is rejoicing and celebrating with them on their brightest days, and yet other times it's crying and sitting with them in their darkest days. Often they're not even looking for words to fix the situation but rather shoulders that are present for them to lean on (Gal. 6:2).

Servant's Eyes

A faithful servant has eyes that look to the Lord for guidance. The pressures of being a good minister, an effective leader, and a disciple maker can be overwhelming. But the good news is that God isn't expecting anyone to do this by their own power. A good servant leader looks to God and his Word for direction (Ps. 121:1–2).

Standing before the Servant King and Hearing Those Words

One thing we must all remember, whether you are currently in ministry or feeling called to be, is that a good servant leader is not a perfect leader. There are no perfect people, and it's not fair to hold leaders to an unfair standard.

At the end of the day, a *good* servant leader is a sinner who has been saved by a *perfect* Savior and has been adopted by a *good* Father. It's always more about who your God is, what your identity is because of him, and the calling on your life to serve from the overflow of that truth. A servant leader is more about who you are than what you do. However, having the desire to faithfully serve people shows the world who you belong to, and it gives an incredible opportunity to introduce the people you are serving to him.

As followers of Jesus, we all desire to hear these words come from the mouth of our King one day: "Well done, good and faithful servant! You were faithful over a few things; I will put you in charge of many things. Share your master's joy" (Matt. 25:23). Notice, he won't say, "Well done, good and faithful pastor, leader, social media influencer, celebrity, executive staff, nonprofit CEO, or denominational president." He will say, "Well done, good and faithful servant." Our ultimate calling is that of a servant. So go and be one for the glory of God.

CHAPTER 9

Balancing Family and Ministry

Juggling is typically a form of amusement reserved for clowns and entertainers. As a youth, I (Scott) learned to juggle and served as a clown (make-up, oversized shoes, and all!), in an outreach ministry on the boardwalk. My skills were limited and I mostly used different types of balls, but the most skilled jugglers can use a variety of things that range from torches to chain saws. To make it even more challenging, some artists add a blindfold or do it while balancing on a unicycle or elevated tightrope. The more perilous the act, the greater the risk and anxiety that come along with it. One slip or drop could result in disaster.

In ministry we can feel like we're juggling personal and leadership responsibilities all while trying to maintain our balance. But for us much more is at stake. The items aren't balls; they're people.

And despite the public nature of ministry, our goal is not to entertain. Most importantly, the risk of a mistake is not limited to our own personal injury. We are called to care for those in our home and those we serve. A misstep can cause us to lose our balance and have everything come crashing down. In the process, we can break hearts, wound souls, shatter people's faith, split churches, and bring shame to the name of our Savior. Although life can sometimes feel like a circus, juggling family and ministry responsibilities is not for clowns.

Anyone who has served in ministry recognizes the difficulty of this juggling and balancing act. Homelife and ministry leadership are intricately related, and our calling elevates the significance of both. Our family is our first ministry field, and our effectiveness as leaders is directly related to our faithfulness in the home. Scripture makes clear: our ability to manage our household is the best indication of our ability to lead God's people (1 Tim. 3:4–5; 1:6). Both require high levels of character, compassion, and competence to shepherd and serve well. Our nuclear family serves as a microcosm of God's family, and a healthy home provides a testimony for others.

The inseparable nature of our family and our ministry require us to balance them together, but their mutual importance can make it difficult to juggle them well without sacrificing one for the other. As you embrace your calling, your ability to balance your family and ministry will ultimately determine your success in both. Therefore, it's important to consider some foundational principles that are essential for our growth and faithfulness.

Praying for Your Family

Although it's never too early to start praying for your future family, before we begin to pray about who we will marry, how many children we will have, and where we will live, we must first consider what Scripture says about family and how it relates to our calling. This can be difficult, especially if it challenges your dreams or conflicts with your desires. But a misstep toward marriage can cause far more hurt and heartache than seasons of waiting or feelings of loneliness.

Interceding for your family starts by *praying through singleness*. In our culture, and more often in our churches, being single is commonly viewed as an indictment against an individual. This is especially true when it comes to evaluating someone for ministry. But Jesus was never married, and neither was Paul. While they both affirmed a high view of marriage (Matt. 19:1–9; Eph. 5:22–33), they also affirmed and honored the deliberate choice of celibacy for the sake of ministry. When his disciples marveled at this level of commitment, Jesus acknowledged its difficulty and the inability for everyone to accept it (Matt. 19:11–12). Paul affirmed its extraordinary nature as well while also explaining the opportunity singleness provides for an undivided focus on and devotion to the Lord (1 Cor. 7:32–35).

While those who are single may not feel like they're in a privileged position, it's important to recognize that singleness is not a commentary on someone's value. As you pursue your calling, praying through singleness should be something you don't automatically dismiss. If you're called to a lifetime of singleness, while there will certainly be struggles, your relationship with the Lord and his satisfying plan for you can provide the highest level of fulfillment for your soul. If you're single for a season or aren't sure what the future holds, you should maintain an open heart and approach this time with unrestrained service to the Lord and commitment to spiritual growth. Praying through singleness can give you a greater passion for your future family as you gain greater clarity.

Praying about your family and discerning God's will for your life also includes *praying for a spouse.* This should not focus so much on pleading with God to bring you someone or interceding for an unnamed individual. But rather, these prayers should focus on shaping your heart's desires to correspond with the character and calling of your potential partner. Practically speaking, this means your call to ministry should determine the attributes you desire in a possible spouse more than the physical appearance, common interests, or mutual friends that would otherwise draw you to them. An authentic relationship with Christ is nonnegotiable, and while it's the most important characteristic, it's certainly not the only one that matters.

A vibrant Christian faith combined with an attractive personality and points of common interest may compel you to pursue a relationship with someone. But being compatible in life does not mean they should become your companion for life. While some debate whether the Lord has "*the* one" for you, there's no doubt that not just "*any*one" will do. It's important for your future spouse to understand your calling and the implications it has for your life. It's equally vital for them not to compromise their own calling just to support yours. As each of you pursue your individual callings, you must prayerfully discern if God is calling you to fulfill his plan together.

This means that you should approach any significant dating relationship with your calling in mind. Before you start seeing someone, you should evaluate whether it has the potential to distract you from pursuing your calling. If you're currently in a committed relationship, you need to have an honest conversation that may require you to take a step back to prayerfully consider your future. And, if you're already married, open and ongoing communication about your calling will be crucial as you prayerfully consider God's next steps for you as a family.

Next to trusting Christ as your Lord and Savior and surrendering to your call to ministry, discerning God's will for you regarding singleness and a future spouse is the most significant decision you'll ever make. Getting married for the wrong reasons or being married to someone who does not fully support your calling can put you in the middle of an impossible tug-of-war that you can never win. Your family and your ministry will constantly be in tension. Inevitably, it will tear you apart, pull you in one direction or another, and can ultimately cause you to lose both. On the other hand, when you and your spouse have complementary callings and share a common passion for Christ, serving his people and sharing the gospel, then your marriage will propel you both forward in fulfilling God's plan.

As you carefully discern God's will for your life, praying about your future family establishes an important precedent that conditions you to intercede for your family down the road. Persistent prayers for our loved ones will play a crucial role in our ability to balance family and ministry. As we pray for our family, God provides the wisdom we need, the strength we depend on, the peace we desire, and the love that binds us together.

Prioritizing Your Family

Giving your family top priority is something everyone affirms. But anyone who's been in ministry can attest to the ongoing tension that exists between ministry responsibilities and family commitments. When our family is not given the time and attention they desire (and deserve), it can cause a strain on a marriage, resentment with children, and bitterness in our hearts. Often our family neglect isn't noticed until it's too late and irreparable harm has already occurred. While no one sets out to mistreat their family, it can happen when we fail to prioritize them.

In order to properly focus on our family, we must first establish a *healthy ministry balance*. Even though we can feel pulled in opposite directions, we must recognize that our calling to ministry and our calling to care for our family are meant to complement each other, not compete with each other. But ministry pressures, busy calendars, the tyranny of the urgent, and devotion to our family can cause emotional and personal tension we must learn how to diffuse.

Balancing family and ministry require us to acknowledge some intrinsic challenges. Personal schedules will always be hectic. In today's rapid-paced culture margin can seem like a luxury, but in ministry leadership it's a necessity. Juggling vocational responsibilities with church gatherings, school activities, and recreational commitments is not unique to those in ministry. However, unexpected and urgent ministry needs can preempt and take precedent over our plans. These may seem disruptive, but we must prepare our hearts, families, and schedules to process them accordingly. When possible, we should look for ways to share ministry responsibilities with other leaders and carefully evaluate the level of immediate attention these situations require. Without room to absorb the unexpected, ministry can take over and suffocate our families.

> We must recognize that our calling to ministry and our calling to care for our family are meant to complement each other, not compete with each other.

Another inherent challenge we can face in balancing family and ministry relates to our compensation. Too many ministry leaders can feel overworked and underpaid. This puts extra stress on our family as we struggle financially while also being physically and emotionally stretched to our limits. These challenges aren't unique to young families in ministry, but it's easy to blame or resent our calling when we find ourselves in these situations. Some of it may require us to adjust our lifestyle and recognize that ministry may involve financial sacrifices. Other situations may require us to look for ways to supplement our income when ministry is unable to fully support our family. There may even be times when we need to have honest conversations with those in leadership to express our needs. Patience, transparency, and a willingness to advocate for our family are all aspects of navigating this balance.

While finding ministry balance is challenging, the blessings of ministry can help provide stability. The joys of ministry involvement, the impact our family can have on others, the flexibility to manage our responsibilities, and the love and support of those we serve can all provide a sense of fulfillment that makes it worth our effort. Open communication with family is essential to safeguard us from misunderstandings or unmet expectations. We should also take the necessary precautions to avoid overcommitting ourselves, adjust our schedules during busy personal seasons, and regularly reassess things to establish a ministry and family balance that honors the Lord and fulfills our calling.

As we strive to find a healthy ministry balance, prioritizing our family also requires us to establish *healthy ministry boundaries*. In addition to scheduling guidelines that can help us maintain a proper balance, we also need to implement important guardrails to keep us from steering into other proverbial ditches. While we must guard our heart above all things (Prov. 4:23), Jesus also taught that we should deal radically with sin and avoid temptations (Matt. 5:29–30). Establishing preemptive safeguards can protect our hearts and our families from unintended, but often avoidable, crises. Ministry boundaries serve as practical guardrails that prioritize our family by avoiding situations and temptations that can easily lead to moral compromise.

Because of the interpersonal nature of ministry, the potential for emotional attachment or inappropriate relationships is always a real and present danger. Vulnerable people who find comfort and affirmation in a respected leader may begin to misread our sincere willingness to help as something more than godly compassion. In our own hearts, the affirmation of others can mix with personal disappointments, weaknesses, or family struggles to create a toxic and combustible combination that makes us susceptible to the enemy's schemes. Establishing personal boundaries that limit the types and times of interaction with the opposite sex is important to safeguard our heart, our family, and our ministry. These boundaries also clearly communicate to our family our full devotion to them and signal to others that we are uninterested and unavailable.

Of course, there are other forms of temptations and moral compromise that we should also safeguard against. We must guard ourselves from allowing our leadership responsibilities to fuel pride that mistreats and manipulates people. These can become patterns that transfer into our home, or the collateral damage of our abusive leadership can impact the way our family is treated. Being accountable to other leaders and welcoming constructive feedback keeps us humble and helps us avoid these pitfalls.

Perhaps the most important boundaries in ministry are spiritual safeguards. Prioritizing our family requires us to honestly evaluate the motives of our hearts for potential blind spots. Sometimes we lean into our ministry because we feel valued or affirmed in ways we may not sense at home. This can cause us to crave validation from our ministry performance and drive us to immerse ourselves in our responsibilities. Other times ministry becomes an escape for domestic struggles we'd rather ignore than address, so we stay busy and classify it as an unwavering commitment to our calling.

Sometimes our motives aren't impure, but we fail to prioritize our family when we gradually become deceived into thinking the ministry demands are seasonal and "things will slow down" after we complete certain projects. When this happens, we ask our families to be patient and understanding, which only leaves them disappointed and frustrated when nothing changes. We can also convince ourselves that our relentless dedication to ministry is for the benefit of our family when, in reality, we're only satisfying our selfish desire for significance and leaving them feeling manipulated and exploited. Regularly communicating with our family, inviting them to share their concerns, and making the necessary adjustments can provide a healthy boundary that guards our hearts accordingly. This type of safeguard will help us prioritize our family as we strive to establish a healthy balance and healthy boundaries in our ministry.

Protecting Your Family

Similar to our responsibility of prioritizing our family, we must also recognize the cautions and challenges in ministry that require us to protect our family. Too many marriages and children of those in ministry have experienced the pain and sorrow of a broken home. Their shattered lives and destroyed ministries are testimonies to the dangerous threats our families face in ministry.

In order to effectively protect our family, we must first adjust to *life in a glass house*. If you can imagine living in a home where every wall and every room is see-through, you can get a sense of what it feels like to serve in ministry leadership. In some ways, there are no places to hide, there is very little privacy, and everyone seems to have open access to your life. While some are courteous enough not to stare, others assume permission to peek into your life and critique everything you say or do. When certain aspects of our lives are scrutinized, we are often left defenseless because explanations would only disclose more intimate details about our families. The constant feeling of watching eyes can create an unspoken pressure to perform, unrealistic expectations, and a defensive posture in our heart that becomes unwilling to trust others and have meaningful relationships. These can be especially felt by our spouse and children.

If we're not careful to guard our family, they can feel exposed. We must learn how to draw the personal and emotional curtains that help our home feel safe and secure. Some of these measures include ongoing practices like limiting family illustrations in our messages and not sharing overly personal details in our conversations. They can also involve planning family meals, outings, and getaways that don't include members of our ministries. These efforts allow us to feel the freedom and joy of being together without any subconscious effort to maintain a level of performance or discretion. It can also be beneficial if we have some close friendships that exist outside of our immediate ministry context. These relationships allow us to emotionally relax while also providing opportunities to let down our guard and openly share concerns, frustrations, or doubts without the subtle fear of repercussions.

Protecting our family also involves embracing *life in God's house.* The call to ministry leadership is typically discerned through our active service and involvement in the local church. Those seasons of discernment are exciting and often invigorate our love for God's people. And when we immerse our immediate family into our church family, we get to enjoy all the blessings that make us one big happy family. But, as we become more invested and involved, we also begin to recognize various family dynamics that can be difficult to navigate.

Some of the challenges involve processing privileged information about our people's personal issues, struggles, and failures. Our
awareness of these private matters can make our relationship with
them awkward and uncomfortable. We must be intentional not to
allow our knowledge of these issues to affect how we view them or
serve them. When it comes to protecting our family, we must also
guard their hearts and minds by determining what's appropriate
to share and how much detail is necessary. Limiting the amount
of information regarding their situation can free our spouse to be
unhindered in their love for that person. However, making them
aware of the circumstances can invite them to join in our prayers
and support of them. This is an important dynamic to discuss with
our family and to determine how we approach the issue.

As we're made aware of people's personal issues, our families
can also begin to shoulder the spiritual weight of their problems.
Emotional fatigue, frustration on their behalf, and physical exhaus-
tion from meeting their needs can affect our family if we don't
learn how to measure our involvement and support. While we are
encouraged to carry one another's burdens, there are also aspects
of the burdens that everyone must bear on their own (Gal. 6:2, 5).

Another challenge to life in God's house is navigating interpersonal conflict among the people we serve. When disagreements arise
between people and families we care about, it's easy to feel caught
in the middle. Helping resolve the issues without taking sides is
not easy. It's also difficult to empathize with someone and, at the
same time, avoid validating their assumptions or accusations against
someone else. As we manage these situations, we must be careful
not to allow our families to become entangled in the disagreements.

We must continue to foster love for our people and not allow their behavior in these scenarios to sour our hearts toward them.

Another protective measure we must take for our families is to guard our children from becoming jaded toward the church. This means we must be careful not to expose them unnecessarily to issues too difficult to process. While we may not discuss these things directly with them, we must be mindful of what they may overhear in our conversations with our spouse or other leaders. This also involves being careful with how we characterize people who are struggling or those who are involved in misunderstandings so that we shape our children's heart with care and compassion rather than contempt and criticism.

The most important aspect of protecting our family is helping our spouse and children understand that their identity is not defined by our position. This can happen when their behavioral expectations are elevated because of our role or when we hold our reputation over their heads when they make mistakes. While others may unfairly evaluate them according to a different standard, we must make every effort to release the weight with our consistent affirmation and appreciation. Providing unquestioned love and support, especially in front of others, can alleviate the pressure our position may cause. Protecting our families by preparing them for life in a glass house and life in God's house is crucial to balancing family and ministry.

Conclusion

Because the relational and circumstantial dynamics of our families and ministries are always changing, balancing them requires constant effort. Like riding a bike without training wheels, a subtle and continual shifting of weight is necessary to keep us from tumbling out of control. It also requires us to keep moving forward and not give up, to learn how to lean into the curves and corners in life and ministry, and to discern when to slow down or speed up according to the different terrains along the way.

Similarly, balancing our family and ministry takes practice and builds on the fundamental principles we've explored in this chapter. Praying about your future family with an open heart toward singleness and a spouse will help cement your convictions and strengthen your commitments regarding God's will for your family life. Prioritizing your family will require you to establish a healthy balance and boundaries to ensure that your dedication to your ministry does not supersede your devotion to your family. And protecting your family involves communicating and working together as you navigate life in a glass house and life in God's house.

Ultimately, family and ministry are a matter of stewardship. God has entrusted both to us, and we must do everything we can to be found faithful as we juggle and balance our roles and responsibilities. May he strengthen us for the task with his wisdom and grace, and may he preserve and protect them both for the sake of his great name.

CHAPTER 10

Persevering in Ministry

In the 1968 Summer Olympics, held in Mexico City, Mexico, John Stephen Akwari ran in the marathon representing Tanzania. At the thirty-kilometer (18.6 miles) mark of a forty-two kilometer (26.09 miles) race, Akwari cramped up due to the high altitude while battling for a position between some runners and fell completely down. He dislocated his knee and injured his shoulder. However, he didn't quit the race. He continued running and finished last among the seventeen competitors who completed the race (seventy-nine had started).

Akwari finished the race over an hour after the top finisher. Most of the crowd had left. The medal ceremony was already over. The sun had set. Astonishingly, Akwari kept running toward the finish line. A television camera crew that had been covering the medal ceremony was sent back to the stadium when they received a message that there was still one more runner about to finish. As Akwari finally crossed the finish line, a cheer came from the small crowd that had remained. When interviewed by the camera crew sent back to the finish line as to why he continued running and didn't quit, he simply said, "My country did not send me five thousand miles to start the race; they sent me five thousand miles to finish the race."

This true story represents in so many ways the reality of what it's like to run the marathon the Lord has called us to. That is exactly what ministry is—a marathon, not a sprint. Also, along the way, we may experience some wounds inflicted on us from those we've been called to serve; however, we still can't quit. Our calling doesn't stop; the race isn't over. After all, the Lord did not save us and call us to ministry only to start the race but to also finish the race. When do we know we've crossed the finish line? When we stand before the King of kings and the words come from his mouth, "Well done, good and faithful servant" (Matt. 25:23).

The hope and encouragement we have for this ministry marathon is that we're not running alone. The Lord himself is with us. He is working through us, he is our power, and he is faithful to see his work in us come to a full completion (Phil. 1:6).

Another subtle part of the 1968 Summer Olympics story speaks volumes and has some unfortunate similarities to ministry. It's the briefly mentioned part of the story where *seventy-nine* runners started the race, but only *seventeen* finished. For whatever reason—whether fatigue, pain, or the extreme conditions produced by the high altitudes of the city—most of the people did not finish the race. Many gave up and walked away. However, this badly injured man was able to finish. He endured pain, suffering, extreme conditions, and he still finished. He ran the marathon and completed it. He accomplished the task. While many quit, he didn't. While most walked away, he crossed the finish line. He persevered.

Anyone can start the race, but only the dedicated will complete it. It's the same with ministry. Anyone can start, but only the faithful driven by a love for Christ and his people will finish the race for the glory of God. Dr. Jason Allen wrote it this way: "Ministry service is glorious, but it can also be uniquely taxing, and only those propelled by a love for Christ and His church survive the long haul."[1] The prophet Isaiah said, "But those who trust in the LORD will renew their strength; they will soar on wings like eagles; they will run and not become weary, they will walk and not faint" (Isa. 40:31).

So that's the question. If we're called to ministry, how do we start well, run well, and finish well to bring honor to the name of Jesus? How do we persevere in this calling of ministry? We intentionally saved this topic for one of the last chapters. Hopefully, you've persevered through the book to make it to this part as we wrap up by talking about how to persevere in ministry for the name, fame, and glory of the One who has called us.

Here are several things to keep in mind.

Learn from Those Who Did It

I (Shane) have recently taken up the hobby of running. Now I realize that just may have made you cringe. Maybe Proverbs 28:1 just came to mind for you: "The wicked flee when no one is pursuing them." Why would anyone run unnecessarily? Well, I've grown to love it and have competed in some 5Ks, 10Ks, and worked up to some half-marathons. When I am training for these races, I want to learn from those who've actually done it. When it comes to learning best practices, I'm not interested in theories. I want to know practical truths from practitioners. Meaning, they live it and they do it.

It's the same in finishing well and persevering in ministry. Learn from those who did it. Now, in crossing the finish line of faith, calling, and ministry, it can sound a little morbid. We're talking about learning from men and women who've passed from this earth into heaven. Death is the only way to cross the finish line because in ministry we don't ever retire; we just graduate. Yes, you may retire from having an official title, but there is no retirement from knowing Jesus and making him known.

So to truly learn from those who did it well, we look to those who've gone before us and are now worshipping around the throne of Jesus. Weird, right? I once heard a pastor say, "I've gotten to where I only want to read dead authors because to learn from them, I want to know how they finished their race." That's not to say we can't learn anything from the living, the young, or even those who may have made mistakes in ministry. However, the point is, if we want to persevere in ministry, then let's look to those who've done it well. Let's learn from them.

One of the greatest to do it was Billy Graham. There is so much to learn from this man, whom God used in massive ways. On February 21, 2018, William Franklin Graham Jr., affectionately known as Billy, graduated from his earthly ministry to go be with

Jesus. He was often called "America's Pastor," and he lived ninety-nine years as a shining example to us all. He wasn't perfect—none of us are—but he was by all appearances and personal stories from close friends and family a leader in love with Jesus and a leader of integrity who ministered faithfully, persevering until the end.

I (Shane) had the honor of hearing the legendary evangelist preach live one time. It was the 2002 Dallas Crusade at Texas Stadium. The stadium was filled to the brim with people, enthusiastic energy, and the power of the Holy Spirit. Billy Graham, at age eighty-three, stood up and preached a clear gospel message with boldness, followed by hundreds, if not thousands of people, pouring onto the field to profess Jesus Christ as their Lord and Savior.

As a young man at the time, I was captivated by this living legend. But even more so, I was captivated by the Savior he proclaimed. It inspired me to learn from this great man for the last twenty years (at the time of this writing). Although I never met him, he taught me many things about preaching, leading, walking in integrity, persevering, and constantly pointing people to Jesus. I believe this great leader is still teaching us many things about what it means to faithfully persevere in ministry. Here are several things we can learn from Billy Graham and others who have actually accomplished it.

Live a Focused Life

Whether or not people believed in the Jesus that Billy Graham preached, everyone knew that he believed it. He had one focus in life: to preach the love of Jesus to a world that desperately needed it. He once said, "God proved his love on the cross. When Christ hung and bled and died, it was God saying to the world, 'I love you.'" He focused on the essentials and wasn't distracted by secondary issues.

Many times the reasons we burn out or chase after things that lead us into a ditch is because it's far too easy to become distracted by things that won't matter a hundred years from now. If we're honest, most of the things that distract us in ministry don't really matter in the moment. If the enemy can't make you fall into sin, he will distract you with silliness. We are here on the earth to know Jesus and to make Jesus known. Just like in a race, if you focus on the wrong things, you'll trip, fall, or run off the track. Focus on Jesus and the purpose of your calling.

Stand with Gospel Boldness

For many years, Billy Graham preached to thousands while standing under a huge banner that quoted Jesus: "I am the way, the truth, and the life." Ministers face a lot of cultural pressure to cower to political correctness, political agendas, and political parties. However, amid a changing culture leaning more and more toward pluralism—a belief that there are many paths that lead to God—Billy Graham never backed down or buckled to the cultural pressures around him. He boldly stood and proclaimed that Jesus is the only way. As Christians and ministers of the gospel, we must be emboldened by this same conviction.

Now, we're not saying that leaders and churches should not involve themselves in cultural conversations, political efforts, and actively stand up for justice. Those are biblical principles and offer incredible opportunities to build relationships, serve people, and share the gospel. However, that's the point. Stand with boldness for the sake of the gospel in all those arenas and opportunities. Everything we do as Christian leaders must be about the gospel. We're not called to be ambassadors for a political party, a social cause, or a cultural agenda. We're called to be ambassadors for Christ (2 Cor. 5:20). Sadly, there are too many stories of people in ministry who started down a path causing them to have political boldness and social boldness, but they lost their gospel boldness. Their agendas began to conflict with the gospel and their ministry calling. So they chose their agenda, and now they're no longer in ministry, or their ministry is no longer about the pure gospel.

Practice What You Preach

Billy Graham was the epitome of integrity. He routinely preached, "If evil were not made to appear attractive, there would be no such thing as temptation." He constantly surrounded himself with safeguards and accountability. There are numerous stories of him having the television removed from his hotel room. People were sent in to check his room before he would enter. In over sixty years of ministry, there were no scandals attached to him. Believers and unbelievers both recognized that his ministry was always in line with his message. He taught us all that our ministry calling is too important and the cost is too high to fall into sin.

Nothing hinders ministry more than hypocrisy, a lack of integrity, and isolation. As Scott and I are getting older and exposed to more leaders, we hear more stories of moral failures that make people leave the race God called them to or, even worse, disqualified them from ministry completely. Almost weekly we hear another tragic story. Many have been close friends.

First and foremost, may we never become so arrogant that we begin to believe it can't happen to us: "Pride comes before destruction, and an arrogant spirit before a fall" (Prov. 16:18). Second, no one wakes up one day and says, "You know what? I think I want to blow up my family and ministry today." So, how does this happen? Why do moral failures happen to people in ministry? Because at some point small compromises crept in, and over time a slow fade began to happen. Then one day they fell to the temptations they promised they never would. They heard of others failing and falling out of the race, and they said to themselves, *That will NEVER be me.* But now here they are—facedown on the track.

Instead of a slow fade away from Christ, holiness, and integrity, ministry leaders must constantly press in. Perseverance requires intimacy with Christ, integrity, and character. Every leader should have accountability and safeguards in place. Lance Witt articulates this well when he says, "Ministry is a character profession. I can't separate my private life from my public leadership. According to Jesus, it is holiness of my private life that gives spiritual power and validation to my public ministry."[2]

Instead, many ministry leaders push away other trusted leaders that challenge them, question them, or offer feedback on their actions. When you do this, you're setting yourself up for failure. (We're not talking about antagonists but trusted, well-intentioned friends and colaborers.) Lean into this. Welcome it into your life and ministry. Practice yourself what you preach to others.

God Does Extraordinary Things through Ordinary People

It's easy to look at Billy Graham as a larger-than-life figure. Titles like *legend*, *spiritual giant*, and *super-Christian* come to mind when you think of him. However, his daughter describes her daddy in a different way through a statement she released after his passing on her Facebook account:

> When I think of him, I don't think of Billy Graham, the public figure. I think of my Daddy. The one who was always a farmer at heart. Who loved his dogs and his cat. Who followed the weather patterns almost as closely as he did world events. Who wore old blue jeans, comfortable sweaters, and a baseball cap. Who loved lukewarm coffee, sweet ice tea, one scoop of ice cream, and a plain hamburger from McDonald's.[3]

God is not looking for all-stars. He already has one: Jesus. He is looking for ordinary people who will follow the all-star Jesus with unwavering hearts. As we discussed in the chapter on serving others, don't seek stardom. Often, when leaders try to build platforms, brands, and popularity, they'll push beyond the limits of Christ's calling into the game of comparison and competition. In those scenarios, it's easy to make compromises and cut corners that they normally never would. But to stay ahead of other leaders or the church across town, you must push harder than Christ is telling you to do. When this becomes your practice, burnout is waiting right around the corner, ready to tackle you out of the race.

Of course, you'll try to spiritualize this drive and ambition by saying, "The more people that know about me, our ministry, or our church can also hear more about Jesus." But if we were to look into our heart of hearts, we'd see something darker at work—just ministry leaders trying to be extraordinary so that people will see how extraordinary they truly are. That is not our calling. Our calling is to show the world how extraordinary Jesus is, not how amazing we are. It's like someone once said, "I'm just a nobody trying to tell everybody about the great Somebody." Keeping a proper view of this truth constantly in front of you will help you persevere.

There Are No Perfect People

When you look up the word *Christian* in a dictionary, you would expect to see a picture of Jesus followed by a picture of Billy Graham. However, although Billy Graham was a godly man, he was not perfect. Dr. Graham often shared about his greatest regret, and that was not spending enough time with his children. He estimated "that he was gone approximately 60 percent of his children's growing up years."[4] Preaching crusades and doing ministry often pulled him away for weeks and months at a time. This is a great reminder that the Savior Billy Graham preached about was the same Jesus he himself needed. This should be an encouragement to us all. No one is perfect, and everyone needs Jesus.

You don't stop needing Jesus and the power of the gospel once you're called to ministry. Leaders aren't perfect. We shouldn't try to be, nor should we present ourselves in that light. As a leader called to ministry, you desperately need Jesus every day. You must constantly press into the gospel work in your life. No matter how long you're in ministry, how many degrees you obtain, or how many people know your name, you never mature past the gospel; you mature in the gospel. To persevere in ministry, you need to preach the gospel to yourself daily.

Most Bible scholars believe 2 Timothy is Paul's last letter of all his New Testament writings, and he chose to write it to young Timothy. You can almost read it like the final words of a spiritual father to his son in ministry. Toward the end of this letter, it's as if you can hear the finality in Paul's voice as these words are being written: "For I am already being poured out as a drink offering, and the time for my departure is close. I have fought the good fight, I have finished the race, I have kept the faith" (4:6–7).

Those are *persevering* words. It's like he knew his finish line was nearby. His ministry race on earth was about to be done. Now he would be waiting to hear the most affirming and satisfying words anyone called to ministry could ever hear from Jesus, "Well done, good and faithful servant! You were faithful over a few things; I will put you in charge of many things. Share your master's joy" (Matt. 25:23).

May that also be our goal—that at the end of our ministry here on earth we would be able to say what Paul said and hear what Paul heard because we persevered for the name, fame, and glory of our great God. He deserves that.

CHAPTER 11

Preparing for Ministry

As a young man discerning his call to ministry, I (Scott) was eager to serve the Lord but didn't immediately have opportunities. During that season, my mentor challenged me to focus on my own spiritual development and life maturity. Instead of praying, "God use me," he encouraged me to pray, "God, make me usable." Now, after more than two decades in ministry, I not only recognize the wisdom in his counsel, I'm still reaping the benefits of what became one of the most fertile and fruitful seasons in my life—the season of preparation.

Preparation typically involves diligence and discipline that the average person would prefer to avoid. Think about it—most people will gladly enjoy an elaborate meal if they don't have to cook it. In sports, most players would love to skip workouts and watching film if they could just go play the game. And who wouldn't choose to just show up and enjoy the vacation if you could get out of packing and planning? But preparation doesn't just happen, and it can't be bypassed. It's necessary. And for those who are called to ministry, it's an essential part of our journey.

Consider the lives of those who were called by God in Scripture. It's easy for us to focus on their triumphs and overlook the intense preparation involved. For example, God's call of Abraham included the promise of a family and nation that wouldn't begin until Isaac was born twenty-five years later. Likewise, the Lord revealed his plan to Joseph as a teenager, but his dreams and God's promises weren't fulfilled until he was reunited with his family more than twenty years later. His season of training included family betrayal, being enslaved, false accusations, and imprisonment, but God used those experiences to equip him and shape his character (Ps. 105:19).

God's plan for Moses was evident by his supernatural protection of him as a child, but he would spend forty years in Midian as a shepherd before God sent him back to Egypt to deliver his people. David was anointed as king as a teenager but didn't ascend to the throne until almost fifteen years later after serving as a shepherd, defeating Goliath, being banished by Saul, fleeing through the desert, and fighting numerous battles. After his dramatic conversion, Paul spent fourteen years exploring his calling as a bivocational preacher prior to his first missionary journey as part of God's call to global missions. Even Jesus, who clearly understood his divine purpose at the age of twelve, didn't begin his full-time public ministry until he was thirty.

When you reflect on these testimonies and what these men endured, you can understand why most people would rather skip the process or may run from their call to ministry altogether. But notice how God worked during the seasons of preparation to deepen their faith, refine their character, develop their skills, and strengthen their resolve. Those seasons were necessary and remind us that in God's plan, waiting time is never wasted time. With this perspective in mind, we can embrace seasons of preparation and commit ourselves to the steps of obedience they require. While everyone's spiritual journey and season of formation is unique, ministry preparation also includes several practical areas we all must consider.

Family Preparation

Regardless of the age and stage of life you're in, when we discern our call to ministry, we all have a responsibility to consider the members of our immediate and extended family. Some will be supportive. Others will be convinced you're forfeiting your future. Some will want to keep you close while others will affirm your willingness to serve anywhere. Learning how to respond appropriately and how to be mindful of their feelings will begin to prepare you to care for your future family. It can also help them recognize and respect your calling, appreciate the sacrifices you will make, and adjust their expectations accordingly. To prepare your family for your call to ministry, two primary principles should guide your approach.

Caring for your family begins with *honoring your earthly parents*. In the New Testament, Paul points to the fifth commandment as the primary instruction for children in relation to their parents (Eph. 6:2; cf. Exod. 20:12). Our responsibility to honor our parents does not depend on their lifestyle or their leadership, even if they act dishonorably (see Gen. 9:18–28). It's also not limited to our childhood years. The genuine nature of our faith is evident by the care and honor we demonstrate for our families (1 Tim. 5:8). This can be especially important to keep in mind as you discern God's will for your life and discuss it with your family.

When you first begin to express a sense of your calling, it may not be well received by the people you love. These can be difficult conversations, but you must recognize that your parents' hesitancy (or even opposition) typically comes from a heart of love that wants what's best for you. While it's possible that your calling may be a threat to their parental pride or undermine their personal goals for you, those typically aren't the driving factors. Concerns like your future financial stability and career path are legitimate questions you should consider. Parents often have a wealth of experience, practical advice, and godly wisdom that can provide you with beneficial insights and a seasoned perspective. Listen to them, be humble while being honest, and don't immediately reject their questions as threats to your calling or a lack of support.

> The genuine nature of our faith is evident by the care and honor we demonstrate for our families.

As they offer counsel, listen openly while also inviting them into your discernment process so they can recognize that this isn't something temporary or emotional. When necessary, disagree respectfully in a way that acknowledges the validity of the issues while also expressing your convictions about God's call on your life. If you have family members who are lost or immature Christians, don't dismiss or disrespect them as you attempt to help them understand what can only be spiritually discerned. Honoring them may be the testimony God uses to work in their lives. Additionally, the care and concern you show for your earthly parents and extended family will help prepare you to love and lead your family in your future ministry.

While you have a responsibility to honor your earthly parents, the ultimate care for your family comes by *obeying your heavenly Father.* The goal of a godly parent's leadership is to teach children how to obey the Lord. Paul's instruction to younger children goes beyond honor and includes obeying their parents (Eph. 6:1). This assumes parents will be leading their families according to the "training and instruction of the Lord" (Eph. 6:4). It does not obligate children to comply with immoral or illegal demands. But God's ultimate goal in this command is not simply parental submission; it's to train children to follow him.

As you develop into a responsible follower of Christ who is no longer under the dependent watchcare of your parents, you must learn to obey God's will for your life and submit to his authority. Paul demonstrated this type of obedient resolve even when loved ones predicted his suffering and pleaded with him to stay (Acts 21:10–14). Abraham exhibited it when he was called to leave his home and extended family for an unknown destination (Gen. 12:1–4; Heb. 11:8–10). God's plan for your life may not correspond with the wisdom of this world. It may not line up with your dreams and desires, much less the ones your friends and family have for you. But his call must take precedent over any competing interest or respected opinions.

Beyond conflicting advice or counsel, obeying your heavenly Father may be difficult for more personal reasons. Sometimes people struggle to trust him if they haven't had trustworthy parents or if family love and acceptance have been conditional. In these scenarios, be careful not to project the mistakes of your earthly parents onto your heavenly Father. He is always reliable, always faithful, and his love for you can always be trusted. As you learn to obey him now, it will condition you to do so in the future when you face opposition or fear of disappointing others.

Financial Preparation

While the subject of money can be uncomfortable, it is an important part of everyone's life that few people are prepared to discuss and even fewer are equipped to manage. Financial planning will be one of the most practical and significant preparations you make for vocational ministry.

If you're young, thinking about finances may seem unnecessary because your income is limited, and your obligations are few. If you're beginning to pursue your education, paying for school and necessities is a primary concern, and everything else seems irrelevant. And if you're on the verge of full-time ministry, chances are you're already navigating important financial decisions, ranging from major purchases and existing payments to your income needs and ministry options. No matter which scenario describes your situation, adopt sound and biblical principles regarding money that can position you to live generously and protect you from some common financial pitfalls that have shipwrecked so many in ministry.

A healthy approach to your finances starts with *avoiding the money trap*. We live in a culture of affluence. It celebrates the extravagant, equates luxuries and necessities, and assigns worth based on wealth. While we may renounce materialism in principle, its widespread acceptance in our society can entice us to pursue worldly comforts and cause us to measure our success according to these ungodly standards. We can easily find ourselves drowning in debt or discouragement.

> God's plan for your life may not correspond with the wisdom of this world. It may not line up with your dreams and desires, much less the ones your friends and family have for you.

Scripture includes multiple warnings regarding wealth, particularly for those in ministry. Jesus clearly taught that it is impossible to serve both God and money (Matt. 6:24). In Paul's pastoral counsel to Timothy, he cautions him, "Those who want to be rich fall into temptation, a trap, and many foolish and harmful desires, which plunge people into ruin and destruction. For the love of money is a root of all kinds of evil, and by craving it, some have wandered away from the faith and pierced themselves with many griefs" (1 Tim. 6:9–10). This passage describes the alluring appeal of wealth, the gradual drift toward it, and the tragic consequences of its pursuit. Although you may not feel susceptible now, because ministry income is typically more modest, financial temptations can actually be stronger for us, especially when combined with other life factors, like the added stress and expenses of a young family.

The frequent nature of financial struggles in ministry is also evidenced by the specific leadership qualification that prohibits materialistic motives (1 Tim. 1:7; 3:3; 1 Pet. 5:2) and Paul's and Peter's indictment of false teachers on this basis (1 Tim. 6:5; 2 Pet. 2:3). In our contemporary culture, so-called "celebrity preachers" and the moral failure of others in ministry leadership have further validated the dangerous appeal of financial gain. It has also caused some people to view ministry leaders through a cynical lens when it comes to money. This unfortunate, but understandable, reputation only heightens our responsibility to avoid any appearance of impropriety. We must guard against potential misunderstanding or false accusations by limiting our involvement with church finances and being careful not to use church resources for personal benefit. Most importantly, financial integrity helps strengthen the credibility of our ministry and provides a greater opportunity to serve and lead others (1 Thess. 2:5).

In addition to avoiding the money trap, exercising financial wisdom also involves *following a money map*. While no one should enter vocational ministry with an expectation of wealth, Scripture does authorize us to provide for our families (1 Cor. 9:6–12; 1 Tim. 5:17–18). As those who benefit from the sacrificial giving of others, we must be good stewards of our resources and take precautionary steps to avoid undermining our ministries with financial mistakes.

Prior to entering full-time ministry, consider some steps regarding finances that can prepare you to start and finish well. Cultivate contentment that pursues godliness, discover satisfaction with the essentials, and find fulfillment in faithful service to Christ rather than worldly comfort (1 Tim. 6:6–8; Phil. 4:11–13). We must also determine in our hearts to value eternal treasures over earthly trinkets (Matt. 6:19–21). Although we may not be tempted by extravagance, we can be easily enticed by amenities within our reach like gadgets, designer brand clothes, or a newer car. While ministry does not keep us from enjoying nice things, we must learn to live within our means.

Practically speaking, we must manage our finances responsibly and avoid debt as much as possible (Rom. 13:8; Prov. 22:7; 1 Thess. 4:11–12). This includes steering clear of credit card debt, other forms of unsecured debt, and, if possible, student loans. Not only is this good stewardship, but debt is also a reason some ministries or missional agencies won't hire or mobilize you. Learning to live on a budget helps protect us from becoming overextended financially. Some people resist the idea of measured spending, but instead of viewing it as a restriction, money management tools provide financial freedom and allow us to live generously and leverage our wealth for God's kingdom (1 Tim. 6:17–19).

As you financially prepare for the ministry, perhaps the most important step you can take is to learn to give sacrificially. Faithful giving through your local church provides support for its ministry needs and is an essential part of church membership. More importantly, sacrificial giving is an expression of your trust in God to provide for your financial needs and is an expression of your thanks to God for meeting our greatest need through the sacrificial gift of his Son (2 Cor. 8:9; 9:6–15). Our call to ministry does not alleviate our responsibility to give; it elevates it. As ministry leaders, we are called to model the generosity made possible through a modest lifestyle that short-circuits any possibility of an accusation of financial mismanagement.

Future Preparation

When you begin discerning your call to ministry, it's difficult to imagine what your future will look like. The broad range of ministry roles and ministry contexts can be exciting to consider. But when it comes to making decisions related to next steps, the seemingly endless number of options creates a maze of pathways that can be disorienting and cause second-guessing. This is especially true when we don't know exactly what ministry role we're preparing for and the type of equipping it requires. Without knowing the specifics, two paths everyone called to vocational ministry must consider are academic training and ministry experience.

> Our call to ministry does not alleviate our responsibility to give; it elevates it.

In order to properly prepare for your future, you must first answer *the education question*. Choosing a college is a difficult decision regardless of your vocational calling. But when you discern your call to ministry, there are additional factors to consider. Some godly people who care about you may encourage you to pursue a nonministry-oriented field of study. On one hand, this pathway can provide you with a skill that can be used as a platform ministry in a missional context or equip you for bivocational ministry. On the other hand, if the rationale behind their counsel is to give you a vocational backup plan, provide financial security for your family, or delay your theological and ministry training until seminary, be careful not to compromise your calling or unnecessarily delay your preparation to pursue an unrelated degree.

Instead, explore the possibility of a Christian college or university that integrates faith and a biblical worldview with all areas of knowledge. You should prayerfully consider schools that are grounded in the truth of Scripture with a missional focus that offer degree programs with specialized training for various fields of work and ministry. Schools like The College at Southeastern[1] design their curriculum to equip students with a well-rounded liberal arts education while pursuing their calling, including offering majors and concentrations designed specifically for students going into vocational ministry. It also offers a vibrant student life experience. Most significantly, you typically can earn academic credit while gaining valuable experience through internships and service opportunities that enhance your ministry preparation.

Likewise, for those who are currently pursuing or have already earned an undergraduate degree, a seminary education is an important choice to consider. While some people dismiss formal theological training as unnecessary, academic preparation equips you with the critical knowledge, leadership skills, and practical tools necessary to fulfill your calling. In addition to biblical and theological study, seminary helps shape your ministry philosophy as you develop important competencies in related fields such as evangelism, spiritual formation, counseling, preaching, hermeneutics, and church history. Although these subject areas can be explored on your own, seminary provides the opportunity to learn from experts in their related fields, exposes you to additional views that strengthen and refine your convictions, and challenges you to study important subjects you would otherwise avoid. And while it may seem superficial, a formal education provides additional credibility. Much like a mechanic's certification or a surgeon's degree, it's easier to trust someone's competency when they've had formal training.

Beyond the academic components, your education experience also equips you with other invaluable aspects of ministry preparation. Learning to balance school assignments, family life, church involvement, and social commitments is a critical part of your personal development that will be crucial for your success in ministry. Life only gets busier as you pursue your calling, and a season of school can provide an education of a different kind by stretching your mental and emotional bandwidth, strengthening your family communication, and teaching you how to prioritize effectively. Your education will also connect you with like-minded students who will become ministry partners and trusted friends that you'll lean on for the rest of your life. Establishing a ministry network with professors, ministry leaders, and classmates will also be some of the ways God works in your life to provide ministry opportunities and partnerships.

In addition to the education question, preparing for your future also involves *the experience factor*. Like any vocational training, some things can't be learned in the classroom; they can only be learned in the field. The same is certainly true in ministry. Prayerfully seeking opportunities to exercise your giftedness and fulfill your calling is something you should actively pursue. It often begins in a volunteer capacity that gives you the chance to explore your options without long-term commitments or expectations. This allows you to further clarify and cement your calling with a firsthand look "backstage."

You should also pursue a place to serve that allows you to be mentored. Personal guidance can provide practical insights to help accomplish ministry goals and complete essential tasks. You also gain wisdom from a seasoned leader who helps you understand why those things matter, how tasks fit within the broader vision of the church or ministry, and how to approach your role from a spiritual, rather than pragmatic, perspective.

In seeking ministry opportunities, some students may decide to take a gap year after high school in order to gain ministry experience and refine their calling. Others may commit to serving in a missional context for a designated period after they graduate from college. The North American Mission Board (NAMB) and the International Mission Board (IMB) are two missions agencies that deploy Christ followers to serve in a variety of contexts in different capacities. The opportunities are designed to help you grow in your walk, gain invaluable experience, and prepare you for a lifetime of vocational service.

Perhaps the best way to be equipped for vocational ministry is to combine your education and experience. Integrating the library with the laboratory often enhances both aspects of your development. The classroom can provide foundational knowledge and teach you practical skills that a ministry opportunity gives you the chance to use. Likewise, ministry involvement can provide you with insights and context that deepen your understanding and help you process what you're learning in school. As you prayerfully consider

God's direction, your education and experience will play a vital role in your present-day growth and your future preparation.

Conclusion

Simply put, the familiar adage is true: "A call to ministry is a call to prepare." The chapters in this book have focused on a variety of spiritual and personal aspects of your preparation. These components are certainly the most crucial facets of your development that will, by God's grace, position you to fulfill your calling. Along with these, other practical elements are also necessary, including preparation related to your family, your finances, and your future.

As you consider the implications of preparing your family, honoring your earthly parents while obeying your heavenly Father are two convictions that must guide your approach. Preparing your finances can be complicated, but learning how to avoid the money trap and follow a money map can position you to live generously while also caring for your family well. And preparing for your future requires you to navigate important decisions regarding your theological education and ministry experience.

In each of these areas, you will certainly need the Lord's wisdom and discernment. While preparing for ministry can be challenging, it can also be extremely rewarding and beneficial. Therefore, we should embrace the challenge of Paul's exhortation to Timothy regarding our calling, our gifts, and our preparation: Practice these things; be committed to them, so that your progress may be evident to all. Pay close attention to your life and your teaching; persevere in these things, for in doing this you will save both yourself and your hearers" (1 Tim. 4:15–16). This season of preparation can be one of the most spiritually fertile and fruitful times in your life. And when handled well, you will reap the benefits throughout your life in ministry.

How to Give an Invitation for Calling Out the Called

We pray that you've deeply enjoyed this book. Our hope is that you'll be both encouraged and challenged to live out your calling of knowing Jesus and making Jesus known, and to *call out the called* to do likewise.

So, what now? What's the next step? We've already discussed the incredible need for more faithful men and women to serve the body of Christ. We're pleading with the Lord of the harvest to raise up more laborers (Matt. 9:37), but we also believe those future laborers are in the harvest. They just need to be called out.

That's the heartbeat behind this book. We believe God hasn't stopped calling people, so we must get back to the business of calling out those he has called. One of the greatest next steps we can make is to return to regularly giving effective gospel invitations with integrity and to regularly include a specific time in those invitations for people to have a chance to surrender to the call of ministry on their life. For some reason we've gotten away from doing this in our local churches. Oh sure, you see it done at student summer camps, conferences, and special events, but we have neglected it in the local church for far too long. Now is the time to return.

However, because of the neglect of public gospel invitations over recent decades, many leaders don't know how to give them anymore. So we couldn't think of a better way to close out this book than to give some practical tips on how to give an effective gospel invitation that includes calling out people to know Jesus but also includes calling out those whom God is calling to ministry and missions. Here are several applicable principles to keep in mind.

Keep It Fueled with Prayer

Pray, pray, and pray some more. You are desperately in need of the Lord to speak through you in a way that pierces hearts. In many churches and events, there are hard hearts sitting and waiting to be broken by the Spirit. There are also hearts that are restless and running from the call of God on their life to surrender to serving him and his bride, the church. Prayer is the fuel for every aspect of the preaching ministry. Only he can break those hardened hearts or surrender those hearts to his calling. Just as you should be covering your sermon or Bible study in prayer, so should you be covering your invitation time in prayer as well (Matt. 9:38).

Keep It Biblical

Every Scripture expects to be preached in the light of the gospel. Every Bible communicator should have expectations of themselves to deliver the gospel every week and to call people to respond to it. Most likely, every time you preach you will have people who are spiritually lost in the crowd, others who know Jesus but need to take the next step of obedience like baptism, joining the church, and repenting of sin, and still others who need to surrender to the calling of God on their life for ministry and missions. Be sure to *tell them how they can be found if they need to be saved as well as how to surrender if they are being called.* Especially in these times of hopelessness, people are looking for hope. And we know hope has a name—Jesus. If you want people to take seriously the challenge of inviting their spiritually lost friends and family to church, then you *must take sharing the gospel seriously. And make a point to let people know on a regular basis that giving their life away to making disciples is the most important thing they can do with their life. Then, give them a chance to be obedient to that call.*

> If you want people to take seriously the challenge of inviting their spiritually lost friends and family to church, then you must take sharing the gospel seriously.

Keep It Short

The invitation to respond to the gospel or to be called out should be short and concise. Get to the point of what you're asking them to do and get there quickly. Our default as communicators is often to ramble when we're short on confidence. The longer we talk about responding, the more confusing we become. One of the best ways to get better at this is preparation.

So spend time preparing for the invitation just as you do for your sermons, messages, or Bible studies. Surely you'd never get up to preach or teach completely unprepared or with no direction of what you're going to say. Obviously, don't do that with your invitations either. Just as you already know where you're going in your sermon, you need to know where you're going in your invitation. Every second is valuable. Use each one wisely.

Keep It Understandable

Be clear in what you're asking them to do. Whether you're calling people to repent of their sins and place their faith in Jesus for salvation, calling people to be baptized, or calling out those whom God has called to ministry, be clear. If you're confusing in what you say, then you will cause confusion in how they respond. Can the teenagers in the room understand clearly what you're asking them to do? Nothing stops people from action faster than confusion. Not too long ago, I saw a sign at an airport that read, "Moving Propellers Rip Off Heads." That message was clear. It definitely caused me to respond and take action by looking for moving propellers.

Keep It Moving to the Next Step

Every gospel proclamation has three responses: surrender, rejection, or a request to hear more. You see all those different responses to Paul's preaching in Athens at the end of Acts 17. For two out of three of those responses, there should be a biblical, short, and understandable way to move to a next step of surrendering to Jesus by hearing more of what that looks like, whether that is a call to salvation or a call to ministry.

Whatever you prefer, just do something, and be clear in what you're asking them to do. The method doesn't matter nearly as much as asking people to respond with faith to the gospel message they just heard or in obedience to being a leader to equip others to know Jesus and make him known. It is imperative, however, that there is a plan for immediate follow-up. Few things are worse than someone surrendering to Jesus or to a call of ministry and no one following up with them.

George Whitefield famously once said, "Others may preach the gospel better than I, but no one can preach a better gospel."[1] It is still true today. Others may be better at presenting the gospel, but no one can present a better gospel. Others may be better at calling out the called than you, but no one has a better calling than you. It is one Spirit, one gospel, one church, one calling.

Jesus told his disciples, "The harvest is abundant, but the workers are few. Therefore, pray to the Lord of the harvest to send out workers into his harvest" (Matt. 9:37–38). As his disciples, he is telling us the same thing today. We wholeheartedly believe the future workers for the harvest are currently in the harvest waiting to be *called out*, waiting to be empowered, and waiting to be equipped.

So go and *call out the called*!

Notes

Introduction

1. Barna Group, "The Aging of America's Pastors," March 1, 2017, https://www.barna.com/research/aging-americas-pastors.

2. Aaron Earls, "How Old Are America's Pastors?," March 9, 2017, https://lifewayresearch.com/2017/03/09/how-old-are-americas-pastors.

3. Barna Group, "The Aging of America's Pastors."

Chapter 1

1. Charles Spurgeon, *Lectures to My Students: Complete and Unabridged*, 1980 ed. (Grand Rapids, MI: Zondervan, 1954), 26–33. Spurgeon's four ways to discern God's call were originally focused on the specific call to pastor/preach. But the indicators and their confirmation are not specific to the particular office and are helpful for a broader understanding of the call to ministry. The terms, summaries, and questions reflect our understanding and application of Spurgeon's thoughts.

2. Spurgeon, *Lectures to My Students*, 26.

3. These three aspects of affirmation are addressed more thoroughly in R. Scott Pace, *Answering God's Call: Finding, Following, and Fulfilling God's Will for Your Life* (Nashville, TN: B&H Academic, 2020).

Chapter 2

1. Michael Todd Wilson and Brad Hoffmann, *Preventing Ministry Failure* (Downers Grove, IL: IVP Books, 2007), 43.

Chapter 4

1. J. Oswald Sanders, *Spiritual Leadership* (Chicago, IL: Moody Press, 1994), 85.

2. Sanders, *Spiritual Leadership,* 86.

3. John Mark Comer, *The Ruthless Elimination of Hurry* (Colorado Springs, CO: Waterbrook Press, 2019), 120.

4. Comer, *The Ruthless Elimination of Hurry,* 122.

5. Quoted in G. Michael Cocoris, *Evangelism: A Biblical Approach* (Chicago, IL: Moody Press, 1984), 108.

6. Andrew Murray, *The Believer's Prayer Life* (Minneapolis, MN: Bethany House Publishers, 1983), 10.

Chapter 5

1. Mark Dever, *Dear Timothy* (Cape Coral, FL: Founders, 2004), 158.

2. Dave Harvey, *Am I Called?* (Wheaton, IL: Crossway, 2012), 153.

3. Jimmy Scroggins and Steve Wright, *Turning Everyday Conversations into Gospel Conversations* (Nashville, TN: B&H Publishing, 2016), 51.

4. Greg Stier, *Gospelize Your Youth Ministry* (Arvada, CO: Dare 2 Share Ministries, 2015), 120.

Chapter 6

1. For an expanded study on the church and spiritual gifts, please see Daniel L. Akin and R. Scott Pace, *Pastoral Theology: Who a Pastor Is and What He Does* (Nashville, TN: B&H Academic, 2017).

2. For a more thorough consideration of how to explore, exercise, and employ your spiritual gifts, please see R. Scott Pace, *Answering God's Call: Finding, Following, and Fulfilling God's Will for Your Life* (Nashville, TN: B&H Academic, 2020).

Chapter 7

1. For an expanded study on the person and work of the Holy Spirit, please see Daniel L. Akin and R. Scott Pace, *Pastoral Theology: Who a Pastor Is and What He Does* (Nashville, TN: B&H Academic, 2017).

2. The Bible describes the Spirit's work as personal acts that include teaching, searching, speaking, interceding, testifying, guiding, and revealing. Our actions toward him are also described in personal terms in that he can be grieved (Eph. 4:30), quenched (1 Thess. 5:19), lied to (Acts 5:3–4), and insulted (Heb. 10:26–29).

3. Charles Spurgeon, *Lectures to My Students: Complete and Unabridged*, 1980 ed. (Grand Rapids, MI: Zondervan, 1954), 186.

4. Gerald L. Borchert, *New American Commentary: John 12–21, Vol. 25B* (Nashville, TN: B&H Publishing, 2002), 122–23.

Chapter 8

1. Jeff Iorg, *The Character of Leadership* (Nashville, TN: B&H Publishing, 2007), 115.

2. Jason K. Allen, *Discerning Your Call to Ministry* (Chicago, IL: Moody Publishers, 2016), 84.

3. Dave Harvey, *Am I Called?* (Wheaton, IL: Crossway Publishing, 2012), 137.

4. Iorg, *The Character of Leadership*, 117.

5. Iorg, *The Character of Leadership*, 137.

Chapter 10

1. Jason K. Allen, *Discerning Your Call to Ministry* (Chicago, IL: Moody Publishers, 2016), 84.

2. Lance Witt, *Replenish* (Grand Rapids, MI: Baker Books, 2011), 53–54.

3. Anne Graham Lotz, in Mark Barrett, "Overcoming Struggles, Billy Graham's Children Are Rooted in Ministry Today," *Citizen Times*, February 25, 2018, https://www.citizen-times.com/story/news/local/2018/02/25/overcoming-struggles-billy-grahams-children-rooted-ministry-today/360965002.

4. Shane Pruitt, "5 Lessons That Billy Graham Taught Us," HomeWord, November 6, 2019, https://homeword.com/jims-blog/5-lessons-that-billy-graham-taught-us/#.YjeWTB17lBw.

Chapter 11

1. The College at Southeastern is the undergraduate program at Southeastern Baptist Theological Seminary located in Wake Forest, North Carolina, http://www.collegeatsoutheastern.com. They also offer specialized programs that consolidate your undergraduate education with a master's degree in an accelerated format that allows students to earn two degrees in related fields of study in a condensed format (i.e., Hunt Scholars Program, a five-year bachelor of arts/master of divinity program).

Conclusion

1. George Whitefield, Grace Quotes, https://gracequotes.org/author-quote/george-whitefield/.

Do you remember when the Holy Spirit drew you into vocational ministry?

The process likely occurred over a season, not just in one moment. Hopefully, someone mentored you and prayed with you as God called you. Now you are the one shepherding the next generation, wondering who God is calling and what you should do next.

Scott Pace, Shane Pruitt and the North American Mission Board (NAMB) want to help you lead the next generation of ministry leaders. Understanding a Calling to Ministry is a free companion to *Calling Out the Called*.

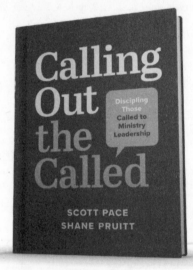

CONTENT COVERS:
What the Bible says about vocational ministry • Discerning your specific calling • How you should prepare for ministry • And more

RESOURCES INCLUDE:
Video downloads from Shane Pruitt • Leader guides for the pastor Devotional guides for the learner • Book recommendations • And more

Go to **CallingOutTheCalled.com** to download this FREE resource